GOLDSMITH'S ANIMATED NATURE

A STUDY OF GOLDSMITH

by

James Hall Pitman

ARCHON BOOKS
1972

Library of Congress Cataloging in Publication Data

Pitman, James Hall, 1896-
  Goldsmith's Animated nature.

  (Yale studies in English, v. 66)
  Reprint of the 1924 ed.
  Thesis–Yale University, 1922.
  Includes bibliographical references.
  1.   Goldsmith, Oliver, 1728-1774. A history of the
earth and animated nature. I. Title: Animated nature.
II. Series.
QL50.G63P5 1972   591   76-179570
ISBN 0-208-01135-8

First published 1924
Reprinted with permission of
Yale University Press, Inc.
in an unaltered and unabridged edition
as an Archon Book
by The Shoe String Press, Inc.
Hamden, Connecticut 06514

Printed in the United States of America

TO MY MOTHER

PREFACE

This book is primarily a study of Goldsmith, in which *Animated Nature* is merely a tool; but, since *Animated Nature* is so little known, I have, as often as possible, used quotations to make my points; moreover, such facts as I have collected serve, I believe, to place it in a light somewhat different from that in which the casual comments of Goldsmith's critics have usually set it. The concentration of emphasis upon Goldsmith, rather than upon his book, has made it necessary to place the detailed consideration of the sources in an appendix.

All references, unless otherwise noted, are to volume and page. Those without a preceding title refer to the first edition (1774) of *Animated Nature*. 'Prior' is James Prior's *Life of Oliver Goldsmith*, London, 1837; 'Boswell, *Life*,' is Hill's edition of Boswell's *Life of Johnson*; '*Works*' signifies J. W. M. Gibbs' five-volume edition (Bohn Library), London, 1881—86.

I owe especial thanks to Professor Chauncey B. Tinker for suggesting this study to me, for allowing me to use his unpublished edition of Boswell's letters, and for much other help and suggestion. Permission to use the newly discovered portrait of Goldsmith by Benjamin West has been most kindly granted by the Ehrich Galleries, of New York City. Finally, I am particularly grateful to Professor Albert Stanburrough Cook for his aid during the printing of the book.

CONTENTS

ILLUSTRATIONS

' The world may be considered as one vast mansion, where man has been admitted to enjoy, to admire, and to be grateful.'

CHAPTER I

FACTS AND CIRCUMSTANCES OF PUBLICATION

Goldsmith is known to the world in general by a poem, a play, and a novel, each notable in its kind, but occupying a place somewhat apart from the bulk of his work. If we are to judge by quantity, his usual medium was not verse, but prose, and his favorite literary form not drama nor prose fiction, but the critical essay. In fact, Goldsmith was, first of all and by necessity, a hack-writer : the great mass of his writing was done in accordance with some previous arrangement with a publisher, and, in some cases, subsequently to full payment for the work. He was a literary drudge first, and an artist afterward. To examine his mind at his ordinary tasks, it is necessary to seek it in a piece of hack work. *Animated Nature* is his most important single enterprise of this sort, and a work whose size is such (the first editions are in eight solid volumes) that the amount of evidence is large enough to insure sound conclusions. A natural history, moreover, written in the compendious manner of eighteenth-century philosophers, and dealing with a large variety of subjects, demanded of its author a wide knowledge—or at least wide reading, some amount of personal observation and of discrimination, and, since the work was intended as a popular treatise, enough literary ability to cast the often obdurate material into attractive form. A glance will reveal the broad scope of *Animated Nature*; that it was popular is proved by the number of editions in the succeeding century. As Goldsmith was here dealing with problems of every sort, and with matter both congenial and uncongenial, and was constructing a work of great size out of more or less ill-assorted material, *Animated Nature* reveals him in a more comprehensive, and perhaps a less flattering way than any other of his works.

Such a study as is here undertaken must consider, and if possible determine once for all, whether *Animated Nature* is a ' mere compilation,' as many critics have asserted, or whether it is really worth attention as a piece of literature. That it is a document important to the study of Goldsmith, no one who has looked at it can doubt. In addition to this, the study, which should add to our knowledge of the contents of Goldsmith's library, and should disclose the secret of his method of putting together a piece of hack work, can not fail to bring out new facts as to his style, and to determine the reasons for its excellence. Finally, these things, in conjunction with a consideration of his moral and philosophic ideas in this book, should enable us to state with more certainty a thing which is still the subject of conjectural controversy—the nature and extent of Goldsmith's intellectual powers.

An History of the Earth, and Animated Nature, by Oliver Goldsmith, in eight volumes, printed for J. Nourse in the Strand, is announced for publication on ' this day ' in the *Public Advertiser* for July 1st, 1774, nearly three months after the writer's death.[1] The work had been five years in preparation, for on February 19, 1769, William Griffin, the book-seller, agreed to pay one hundred guineas a volume for it, with the understanding ' that Dr. Goldsmith is to set about the work immediately, and to finish the whole as soon as he conveniently can.'[2] In 1771 Goldsmith mentioned to

[1] Goldsmith died April 4, 1774.
[2] *Works* 1. 484.

Langton that the work was about half done;[1] and on June 27, 1772, he acknowledged the receipt from Griffin of £840, the whole amount due him,[2] although he had already been paid £500 by September, 1769.[3] Griffin, however, did not publish the book. In 1772 he sold his interest to John Nourse;[4] and, though in 1774 he was desirous of regaining at least a partial proprietorship,[5] there is no evidence that he obtained any share. Nourse was apparently patient and considerate in waiting for the work to be finished : Goldsmith thanks him for his ' *over* payment,' and mentions a contemplated extension of the natural history, in which enterprise he wants the bookseller to share.[5] Nourse did not lose by his kindness, since the book was popular, and he published a second edition in 1779.[6] I count twenty editions and abridgments, the latest dated 1876, in the catalogue of the British Museum Library, and know of two others.[7] The only translation I have yet found is in Welsh.[8]

As the full title implies, *Animated Nature* is not merely an account of living creatures, but a description of the earth itself. Therefore the first volume is devoted to what would to-day be called physical geography. In this Goldsmith is following his master, Buffon, though, not having, like Buffon, a theory to prove, he treats the material in a somewhat different way. We have a

[1] Letter to Langton, Sept. 7, 1771: *Works* 1. 461.

[2] Receipt: *Works* 1. 485.

[3] Receipt: *Works* 1. 486.

[4] Prior 2. 504. I can not locate Prior's evidence for the statement of this date.

[5] Letter from Goldsmith to Nourse, Feb. 20, 1774: *Works* 1. 473.

[6] Copy in the New York Public Library.

[7] Philadelphia, 1823, five volumes, ' with corrections and additions,' in the Yale Library; and London (J. F. Dove), 1828, three volumes, in my possession.

[8] Catalogue of British Museum Library.

general survey of the globe ' from the light of Astro-
nomy and Geography,' a review of several theories of
its formation, then descriptions and discussions of its
internal structure, of its surface, of its waters, of the
air, of volcanoes, earthquakes, winds, meteors (i. e.,
atmospheric phenomena of all kinds), and many other
allied matters. The second volume, also inspired by
Buffon, takes up the discussion of animals in general,
and of man in particular, so that we find such chapter-
headings as 'A Comparison of Animals with the Inferior
Ranks of Creation,' ' Of Sleep and Hunger,' ' Of Old
Age and Death,' ' Of the Varieties of the Human Race,'
' Of Monsters,' and the like. The remaining part of the
work is devoted to animals, discussing, first, quadrupeds,
then birds (volume 5 and part of 6), fishes (the rest of
volume 6, and a small part of 7), frogs, lizards, and
serpents (only about 150 pages), and insects. More than
half of the eighth volume is occupied by an impressive
index, which, for all its size, is shockingly incomplete.

Regarding the actual composition of the book there
is little record. Dr. M'Veagh M'Donnell told Prior [1] of
being befriended by Goldsmith, and even employed by
him ' for a time . . . to translate passages from Buffon,
which was abridged or altered according to circumstances, for his Natural History.' Another assistant,
whom he employed to look up some facts about China,
proved far from satisfactory, and was dismissed with
a guinea. Indeed, Goldsmith seems to have found it
difficult to use assistance in his work. We are told
(though without proofs) that he once employed an
amanuensis, but ' found himself incapable of dictation ;
and after eying each other some time, unable to
proceed, the Doctor put a guinea in his hand, and

[1] Prior 2. 342 ff.

sent him away.' [1] Boswell reports that on Friday,
April 10, 1772,

> Goldsmith told us, that he was now busy in writing a natur-
> al history, and, that he might have full leisure for it, he had
> taken lodgings, at a farmer's house, near to the six mile-stone,
> on the Edgeware road, and had carried down his books in
> two returned post-chaises. He said, he believed the farmer's
> family thought him an odd character, similar to that in which
> *The Spectator* appeared to his landlady and her children:
> he was *The Gentleman*. Mr. Mickle, the translator of *The
> Lusiad*, and I went to visit him at this place a few days after-
> wards. He was not at home; but having a curiosity to see
> his apartment, we went in and found curious scraps of des-
> criptions of animals, scrawled upon the wall with a black
> lead pencil. [2]

Prior, sixty years later, found this farmer's son still
living, who remembered Goldsmith, and said that,
having preserved these scrawls for many years, his family
had been forced to remove them in making some repairs:

> It appears that though boarding with the family, the Poet had
> the usual repasts commonly sent to his own apartments, where
> his time was chiefly spent in writing. Occasionally he wandered
> into the kitchen, took his stand with his back towards the
> fire apparently absorbed in thought, till something seeming to
> occur to mind he would hurry off to commit it, as they sup-
> posed, to paper. Sometimes he strolled about the fields, or
> was seen loitering and musing under the hedges or perusing
> a book. More frequently he visited town, and remained absent
> many weeks at a time, or paid visits to private friends in other
> parts of the country.
>
> In the house he usually wore his shirt collar open in the
> manner represented in the portrait by Sir Joshua. Occasionally
> he read much at night when in bed; at other times when
> not disposed to read, and yet unable to sleep which was not

---

[1] John Pugh, *Remarkable Occurrences in the Life of Jonas Hanway, Esq.* 223, 224. London, 1787. Frankfort Moore misquotes
this title as *James Hanway*.

[2] *Life* 2. 208-209.

an unusual occurrence,[1] the candle was kept burning, his mode
of extinguishing which when out of immediate reach was
characteristic of his fits of indolence or carelessness; he flung
his slipper at it, which in the morning was in consequence
usually found near the overturned candlestick, daubed with
grease.[2]

Besides this, a passing reference in *Animated Nature* [3]
to an incident which occurred ' while I was writing this
history in the county of Essex ' shows us that he must
have stayed for a time also in the country on the opposite side of London, though I find none of his friends
taking cognizance of it.

Cradock, one of Goldsmith's best friends, ' particularly recollected ' that

when Goldsmith was near completing his *Natural History,*
he sent to Dr. Percy and me, to state that he wished not to
return to town, from Windsor, I think, for a fortnight, if we
would only complete a proof that lay upon his table in the
Temple. It was concerning birds, and many books lay open
that he occasionally consulted for his own materials. We met
by appointment; and Dr. Percy, smiling, said, ' Do you know
anything about birds ? ' ' Not an atom,' was my reply : ' do
you ? ' ' Not I,' says he, ' scarce know a goose from a swan :

[1] Cf. 2. 136 : ' Man finds it more difficult than any other animal
to procure sleep: and some are obliged to court its approaches for
several hours together, before they incline to rest. It is in vain
that all light is excluded ; that all sounds are removed ; that warmth
and softness conspire to invite it ; the restless and busy mind still
retains its former activity; and Reason, that wishes to lay down
the reins, in spite of herself, is obliged to maintain them. In this
disagreeable state, the mind passes from thought to thought,
willing to lose the distinctness of perception, by increasing the
multitude of the images. At last, when the approaches of sleep
are near, every object of the imagination begins to mix with that
next it ; their outlines become, in a manner, rounder ; a part of their
distinctions fade away ; and sleep, that ensues, fashions out a dream
from the remainder.'

[2] Prior 2. 332-333, who gives additional details.

[3] 3. 330.

Pl. II. Pag.12.

LE ZEBRE. *Fig. 1. vûe de face. Fig. 2. vûe de dos.*

Buffon's *Histoire Naturelle* 12. 11

however, let us try what we can do.' We set to work, and
our task was not very difficult. Some time after the work
appeared, we compared notes, but could not either of us re-
cognize our own share.[1]

Indeed, Goldsmith's friends in the main seem not to
have taken the embryo natural history very seriously.
Boswell records only one conversation—and a somewhat
flippant one—on the subject.[2] Johnson, of course, with
his usual acumen, knew what to expect. ' Sir,' said he,
' he has the art of compiling, and of saying everything
he has to say in a pleasing manner. He is now writing
a Natural History and will make it as entertaining as
a Persian Tale.'[3] Beyond such scattered references,
there is no indication that Goldsmith's friends heard
much about his scientific struggles. For all his reputed
conversational carelessness, he could apparently be very
close-mouthed about his own affairs.

He was, however, grappling with what must have
been a disheartening, as well as a difficult task. Since
the money for it had already been paid, the book must
be finished as soon as possible. The first part, too,
was much easier to write, because there was little more
to do than tread the path Buffon had already mapped
out; in the latter part, at a time when he must have
had very little zest for the work, there was no such
trustworthy guide to follow. That it was completed
at all is a credit to Goldsmith's sense of duty. He
wrote to Langton in 1771 :

> The Natural History is about half finished, and I will shortly
> finish the rest. God knows I am tired of this kind of finishing,
> which is but bungling work, and that not so much my fault
> as the fault of my scurvy circumstances.[4]

[1] Cradock, *Memoirs* 4. 281.
[2] *Life* 2. 266-267.
[3] *Life* 2. 273.
[4] Letter mentioned above: *Works* 1. 161.

Poverty is not the best assistant in research.   The books which required two post-chaises for their transportation were not come by for nothing.   In the preface to *Animated Nature* he says :

> But what shall I say to that part, where I have been left entirely without his [Buffon's] assistance ?   As I would affect neither modesty nor confidence, it will be sufficient to say, that my reading upon this part of the subject has been very extensive ; and that I have taxed my scanty circumstances in procuring books which are on this subject, of all others, the most expensive.[1]

If there is any merit in *Animated Nature*, it surely does not come from the joy of the author in the book's creation.   This is hack work, if there ever was any.

Nevertheless, natural history was far from being distasteful to Goldsmith, or unsuited to his capacity. His medical knowledge, though certainly not extraordinary, was sufficient to give him a very real interest in science, particularly when it concerned living creatures.   His European peregrinations had given him an opportunity to see nature outside of the British Isles. That he could be observing when he wished is proved by his early essay on the spider, in No. 4 of the *Bee* (Oct. 27, 1759), the substance of which he incorporated into *Animated Nature*.[2]   Then, too, despite that common sense which characterizes most of his essays, Goldsmith, by a sort of natural sensibility, was inclined to a profound, though sometimes almost ludicrous sympathy with animals—a trait which fitted in well with the fashionable sentimentalism of the day.   He had, moreover, in 1763 and later, been actually employed by

---

[1] 1. xii.

[2] 7. 249 ff.   Goldsmith was never slow to save himself labor by using his previous work over again, if it fitted well into the piece under his hand.

Newbery to write the preface and introductions to Brookes' *New System of Natural History*, and otherwise retouch it.[1] The idea of writing *Animated Nature* may at that time have been already conceived.

It must be remembered that Goldsmith considered the work as a literary, not as a scientific, venture. His preface states the case quite clearly:

> The delight which I found in reading Pliny, first inspired me with the idea of a work of this nature. Having a taste rather classical than scientific, and having but little employed myself in turning over the dry labours of modern system makers, my earliest intention was to translate this agreeable writer, and by the help of a commentary to make my work as amusing as I could. Let us dignify natural history never so much with the grave appellation of a *useful science*, yet still we must confess that it is the occupation of the idle and the speculative, more than of the busy and the ambitious part of mankind. My intention, therefore, was, to treat what I then conceived to be an idle subject, in an idle manner; and not to hedge round plain and simple narratives with hard words, accumulated distinctions, ostentatious learning, and disquisitions that produced no conviction. Upon the appearance, however, of Mr. Buffon's work, I dropped my former plan, and adopted the present, being convinced by his manner, that the best imitation of the ancients was to write from our own feelings, and to imitate Nature.
>
> It will be my chief pride, therefore, if this work may be found an innocent amusement for those who have nothing else to employ them, or who require a relaxation from labour. Professed naturalists will, no doubt, find it superficial; and yet I should hope that even these will discover hints and remarks gleaned from various reading, not wholly trite or elementary. I would wish for their approbation. But my chief ambition is to drag up the obscure and gloomy learning of the cell to open inspection; to strip it from its garb of austerity, and to show the beauties of that form, which only the industrious and the inquisitive have been permitted to approach.

[1] Prior 1. 469, and receipts: *Works* 1. 480, 483.

It can not be too much emphasized, then, that *Animated Nature* is in no sense, and was never intended to be, a scientific work. The whole preface is an extremely straightforward exposition of its merits and its limitations. The moderns in this field, says Goldsmith, have been concerned preëminently with systems, and have, in general, done little more than write dictionaries, which to the expert are helpful because, the ' tedious, though requisite part of study ' being attained,

> nothing but delight and variety attend the rest of his journey. Wherever he travels, like a man in a country where he has many friends, he meets with nothing but acquaintances and allurements in all the stages of his way. The mere uninformed spectator passes on in gloomy solitude ; but the naturalist, in every plant, in every insect, and every pebble, finds something to entertain his curiosity, and excite his speculation.

The ancients seem to have had a different idea of what constituted a natural history :

> They contented themselves with seizing upon the great outlines of history ; and passing over what was common, as not worth the detail, they only dwelt upon what was new, great, and surprising, and sometimes even warmed the imagination at the expence of truth.[1]

The only modern who has really combined the two methods successfully is Buffon ; but, unfortunately (at this time), he has advanced only through the quadrupeds. Here he so far indulges his dislike of arbitrary system that he sets down the animals almost as they happen to occur to him. Goldsmith feels that this is a step too far in the opposite direction, and plans a compromise :

> My aim has been to carry on just so much method as was sufficient to shorten my descriptions by generalizing them,

---

[1] The reader of *Animated Nature*, despite manifest falsities and exaggerations, is rarely led to think that Goldsmith admitted these without authority, merely for the purpose of enlivening the account.

and never to follow order where the art of writing, which is
but another name for good sense, informed me that it would
only contribute to the reader's embarrassment.

Goldsmith had assumed substantially the same attitude
eleven years before, in his introduction to Brookes'
Natural History.[1] This 'art of writing, which is but
another name for good sense,' is evident throughout
Animated Nature, but must have been most frequently
called into play in the latter part, in which the materials,
not coming from so homogeneous a source as Buffon,
called for real formative power on the part of the writer.
Goldsmith was fully aware that it was this latter part
that gave his work any scientific value beyond that of
a superficial compilation :

> In consequence of this industry [in gathering materials for
> the latter portions], I here offer a work to the public, of a kind,
> which has never been attempted in ours, or any other modern
> language that I know of. The ancients, indeed, and Pliny in
> particular, have anticipated me in the present manner of
> treating natural history. Like those historians who describe
> events of a campaign, they have not condescended to give
> the private particulars of every individual that formed the
> army ; they were content with characterizing the generals, and
> describing their operations, while they left it to meaner hands
> to carry the muster-roll. I have followed their manner, re-
> jecting the numerous fables which they have adopted, and
> adding many improvements of the moderns, which are so
> numerous, that they actually make up the bulk of natural history.

Animated Nature, then, while not positively scientific,
is, so far as its author can make it, at least not erroneous.
Goldsmith knew his limitations, and shaped his work
accordingly. As to the result, Johnson was right : Goldsmith's art of compiling made the book as entertaining
as a Persian Tale—and more lastingly so ; few Persian
Tales go through more than twenty editions, or are
deemed worthy of translation into Welsh.

[1] *Works* 5. 88 ff.

b

CHAPTER II

SOURCES OF *ANIMATED NATURE* [1]

There is, I think, no reason to doubt Goldsmith's
statement that ' delight in reading Pliny ' first suggested
to him the idea of a work on natural history; but the
succeeding one, that ' upon the appearance . . . of Mr.
Buffon's work, [he] dropped [his] former plan,' seems
a little exaggerated, since, at the time of the appearance
of Buffon's first volumes in 1749, he was probably
occupied with his more material affairs, and could have
been thinking little about literary matters. Allowing,
then, for the perhaps pardonable exaggeration of the
preface to a piece of hack work, we may suppose that,
although he no doubt felt an occasional interest in
natural history during the fifties, he made no effort to
turn this interest to professional advantage until he was
employed to patch up Brookes' *Natural History* in 1763.
From this time forth, however, we may say that the
plan of *Animated Nature* was fairly well formed in
Goldsmith's mind. Between the two books there is
little change in his attitude toward nature and toward
science in general, though of course *Animated Nature*
amplifies the expression of both. I examined Brookes'
work, suspecting that it must have had a considerable
influence upon *Animated Nature*, but found practically
no relation between the two. The plan of Brookes,
except for the larger divisions, is utterly different from

---

[1] For list of sources and notes upon them, see Appendix.

that of Goldsmith. The pictures of the earlier work,
which I thought, before seeing them, might have
suggested those in *Animated Nature,* have no resemblance
to Goldsmith's. Goldsmith did not even use Brookes'
facts, for he mentions him only thrice by name, and,
of these references, one is cited only to be refuted.

At the first glance, *Animated Nature* seems to be
a work of tremendous erudition. Footnotes, often referring to volume and page, are plentiful throughout,
particularly, however, in the first four volumes, and the
pages bristle with other authorities; my first collection
of Goldsmith's citations amounted to hundreds of different names of writers on every possible subject that
could be worked into a natural history; but it soon
became evident that these were no indication of Goldsmith's knowledge of the books in question. He appro-
priates his footnotes from Buffon and his other books
of reference as freely as he takes information concerning
the animals he is discussing; but, while he is generally
careful to give some authority for his facts, he seems
to consider himself under no obligation to verify such
a reference of Buffon's as '*Description Historique de
Macaçar,*' or ' *Labat, Relat. de l'Afrique Occident.,*' or
even to mention that he cites it on the authority of
Buffon. The tracing of these vicarious sources soon
reveals the fact that Goldsmith's real sources were
surprisingly few, particularly in the first half, where he
is following Buffon. The latter half is drawn from a
somewhat larger number.

In general, the authentic sources are of three kinds :
first, works like those of Linnæus, Gesner, or Boyle,
whose object is purely scientific, or like Buffon's, which
aims to combine science with elegant amusement;
secondly, travels and voyages, which, though their purpose is not primarily scientific, yet contain much de-

scription of animals and of natural phenomena; and
thirdly, the ancient writers, who serve to provide em-
bellishing details and anecdotes, rather than scientific
information.   Aside from these might be mentioned the
purely literary allusions which a man of letters could
scarcely exclude from his writing.   Thus we find him
quoting and translating two lines of Ovid, citing Aristophanes (with the Greek in a footnote), alluding to
Cicero, to the *Georgics*, and to Hesiod, and, more than
once, to hearty Apicius, 'suffocating fish in Cartha-
ginian pickle,' for example; while, of our English writers,
he quotes Shakespeare twice, does not miss Milton's
Satan when he discusses the cormorant, and wonders
whether a hypothetical 'natural' man imagined by
Buffon can be inspired by Milton's Adam, relates the
pathetic story of a whale's maternal love from Waller's
'beautiful poem of the Summer Islands,' mentions
Thomson, quotes Pope and approves his description of
mountains, translates some of Addison's Latin verses,
and even brings in Sir Thomas Browne, 'who expected
to be able to produce children by the same method
as trees are produced,' in connection with the polypus,
which, being multiplied in this manner, makes it possible that 'every philosopher may thus, if he pleases,
boast of a very numerous, though, I should suppose,
a very useless progeny.'   But such allusions, though
interesting in the mass, as showing Goldsmith's method
of lightening dull details of natural history by flashes
of literary illustration, are of little individual importance.

Of the ancient naturalists, Goldsmith almost certainly
knew Aristotle's writings on natural history, perhaps
in a Latin translation, and was acquainted with Ælian's
De Natura Animalium, whence he inserts nearly two
pages of translation concerning the ferocious dogs of

India in the time of Alexander, and perhaps also with his curious collection of anecdotes, the *Varia Historia*, though Goldsmith's references to this may be at second hand. In this case, too, it is unnecessary to suppose that he knew the original Greek, since there were several Latin translations, and of the *Varia Historia* an English one also. I may say here, however, that Goldsmith's knowledge of Latin, at least, seems unimpeachable. In addition to these writers there occur references to many others, but they are usually slight, and often of such a nature that they may easily have been inserted from hearsay, or culled from more modern books, so that it is not always possible to come to an opinion as to whether or not Goldsmith himself knew the work in question. The most considerable ancient source is, of course, Pliny's *Natural History*; but strangely enough, in view of the importance Goldsmith makes this work assume in connection with the genesis of *Animated Nature*, he mentions Pliny by name, if I have made no error, only twenty-five times in the whole eight volumes, and usually these references are nothing but passing remarks. To ignore Pliny as an important element in the book, merely on this ground, would be unsound, however. The facts or pseudo-facts provided by Pliny would naturally have been superseded by later investigation; but the fact that one can really read *Animated Nature* from cover to cover with far less weariness—and certainly less boredom—than must be suffered in reading one of the *Bibliothèque Bleue's* prose romances, is, I think, in no small part due to Goldsmith's desire to arouse in his readers, also, 'the delight which [he] found in reading Pliny.'

He does, however, admit Pliny and the other ancients as of equal authority with the moderns when it seems to him that they are speaking from observation or real

knowledge, instead from a too exuberant or fearful
imagination. He is fully aware of their leaning toward
exaggeration, but excuses them somewhat patronizingly,
in true eighteenth-century style:

> The ancient poets and historians speak of [whirlpools] with
> terror; they are described as swallowing up ships, and dashing
> them against the rocks at the bottom: apprehension did not
> fail to add imaginary terrors to the description, and placed
> at the centre of the whirlpool a dreadful den, fraught with
> monsters whose howlings served to add new horrors to the
> dashings of the deep. Mankind at present, however, view
> these eddies of the sea with very little apprehension; and
> some have wondered how the ancients could have so much
> overcharged their descriptions. But all this is very naturally
> accounted for. In those times when navigation was as yet
> but beginning, and the slightest concussion of the waves
> generally sent the poor adventurer to the bottom, it is not to
> be wondered at that he was terrified at the violent agitations
> in one of these. When his little ship, but ill-fitted for opposing
> the fury of the sea, was got within the vortex, there was then
> no possibility of ever returning. To add to the fatality, they
> were always near the shore; and along the shore was the only place
> where this ill provided mariner durst venture to sail. These were,
> therefore, dreadful impediments to his navigation; for if he at-
> tempted to pass between them and the shore, he was sometimes
> sucked in by the eddy; and if he attempted to avoid them out
> at sea, he was often sunk by the storm. But in our time, and in
> our present improved state of navigation, Charybdis, and the
> Euripus, with all the other irregular currents of the Medi-
> terranean, are no longer formidable. Mr. Addison not attending
> to this train of thinking, upon passing through the straits of
> Sicily, was surprised at the little there was of terror in the
> present appearance of Sylla [*sic*] and Charybdis; and seems to
> be of opinion, that their agitations are much diminished since
> the time of antiquity. In fact, from the reasons above, all
> the wonders of the Mediterranean sea are described in much
> higher colours than they merit, to us who are acquainted
> with the more magnificent terrors of the ocean.[1]

[1] I. 265 ff.

The ancients must not be disbelieved, however, merely because they are the ancients, especially when most of them agree upon a fact, since their agreement (in this particular case, upon the generosity and tenderness of the lion) shows 'that there must be some foundation for the general belief in its good qualities; for mankind seldom err when they are all found to unite in the same story.' [1] Nevertheless, in general, 'the descriptions of Aristotle and Pliny, though taken from life, may be considered as fabulous, as their archetypes are no longer existing.' [2] Besides, as we learn from the Introduction to *A Survey of Experimental Philosophy* : [3]

> The ancients seem to have been but little acquainted with the arts of making experiments for the investigation of natural knowledge. It is true, they treasured up numberless observations, which nature offered to their view, or which chance might have given them an opportunity of seeing; but they seldom went farther than barely the history of every object: they seldom laboured, by variously combining natural bodies, if I may so express it, to create new appearances, in order to afford matter for speculation.

Thus, though in 'diving into the secret recesses of nature, they read the book as it lay before them, but . . . read with great assiduity,' yet it is to the moderns we must go for the bulk of our trustworthy information.

As early as 1763, in the introduction to Brookes' *Natural History*, Goldsmith displayed a very tolerable knowledge of the standard works on the subject. He speaks familiarly [4] of Aldrovandus, 'the most laborious,

[1] 3. 232.
[2] 3. 136.
[3] *Works* 5. 145.
[4] One can never be sure, however, that these confident expressions of Goldsmith denote first-hand knowledge. This one, for example, seems to come from Buffon 1. 26: 'Aldrovande, le plus laborieux et le plus savant de tous les Naturalistes, a laissé après

as well as the most voluminous among the moderns,'
of Gesner and Johnston, who, ' willing to abridge the
voluminous productions of Aldrovandus, have attempted
to reduce Natural History into method,' of Klein, and
Linnæus, and Ray, and Derham, of Swammerdam and
Réaumur in the realm of insects, Edwards in that of
birds, and, finally, of Buffon. These are, with some
relatively unimportant additions, the sources also of
Animated Nature. But, between the dates of Brookes'
history and his own, Goldsmith became much better
acquainted with these books, and in *Animated Nature*
makes candid and positive statements as to what he
conceives to be the proper method of treating the
subject.   In the first place, he considers mere speculation
a waste of time, for ' as speculation is endless, so it is
not to be wondered at that all these [philosophers]
differ from each other, and give opposite accounts of
the several changes, which they suppose our earth to
have undergone.' [1] ' It is finely remarked by Bacon,
that the investigation of final causes is a barren study;
and, like a virgin dedicated to the Deity, brings forth
nothing.' [2] ' It is amazing . . . to trace the progress
of a philosophical fancy let loose in imaginary specula-
tions ; ' but ' these reveries generally produce nothing ;
for, as I have ever observed, encreased calculations,
while they seem to tire the memory, give the reasoning faculty perfect repose.' [3] ' It is not from any speculative reasonings, upon a subject of this kind, that in-

un travail de soixante ans, des volumes immenses sur l'Histoire
Naturelle,' and is, no doubt, a conscious quotation ; but by the
time he came to write *Animated Nature*, he was so saturated with
Buffon's ideas and expressions that I fully believe he often used
them without realizing their source.

[1] I. 22.

[2] I. 20.

[3] I. 106, 107.

formation is to be obtained; it is not from the disputes of the scholar, but the labours of the enterprising, that we are to be instructed in this enquiry.' [1]

In the second place, Goldsmith draws a sharp distinction between ' experimental philosophy ' and ' natural history.' As he shows us in the Introduction to *A Survey of Experimental Philosophy*, that subject is altogether useful and necessary :

> The first efforts of [man newly introduced into the world] would be to procure subsistence, and, careless of the causes of things, to rest contented with their enjoyment. The next endeavor of such a creature would be to know by what means he became blest with such a luxuriance of possession ; he feels the grateful vicissitudes of day and night—perceives the difference of seasons—he finds some things noxious to his health, and other grateful to his appetite : he would therefore eagerly desire to be informed how these things assumed such qualities, and would himself, from want of experience, form some wild conjecture concerning them. . . . Succeeding observations would, however, soon contradict his first prejudices, and he would begin to treasure up a history of the changes, that every object served to work either upon himself or upon each other. . . . From hence [by combining such observations] new systems would be erected, more plausible indeed than those already made by savage man, but still, from a want of a sufficient number of materials, extremely defective : so that fancy would be obliged to supply the greatest share of the fabric. . . . At length, after frequently experiencing the futility of system, man would be obliged to acknowledge his ignorance of the causes of most appearances, and now, grown modest, would set himself down, not only to collect new observations, but, in a manner, to torture nature by experiments, and oblige her to give up those secrets, which she had hitherto kept concealed; [2] . . . and, by . . . uniting the whole, man

---

[1] 2. 258.

[2] Cf. *Animated Nature* 1. 309 : ' [The naturalist] gives an history of Nature, as he finds she presents herself to him ; and he draws the obvious picture; [the experimental philosopher] pursues her with close investigation, tortures her by experiment to give up her secrets, and measures her latent qualities with laborious precision.'

would at last begin to discover the simplicity of nature under all her seeming variety.

Such is the progress of natural philosophy in the human mind, which, from enjoyment, proceeds to conjecture; from thence to observation of facts, which, from their paucity, give birth to hypothetical system, which is succeeded by experimental investigation, and this at length gives rise to the true experimental system, which, though still defective, is yet built upon the surest foundation.[1]

But 'all knowledge is pleasant only as the object of it contributes to render man happy;'[2] useless experiments, then, are not justifiable. 'Many have been the animals that idle curiosity has tortured in the prison of a receiver, merely to observe the manner of their dying.'[3] Another type of useless experiment is, for example, the scientifically successful attempt to sweeten sea-water: 'In this state, therefore, have the attempts . . . rested; the chymist satisfied with the reality of his invention; and the mariner convinced of its being useless.'[4] And of an even less useful sort is such as the one by which it was proposed to discover the rate of increase in the saltness of the sea: 'All this may be fine; however, an experiment, begun in this century, which is not to be completed till some centuries hence, is rather a little mortifying to modern curiosity; and, I am inclined to think, the inhabitants round the Caspian sea [where it was proposed to try the experiment] will not be apt to undertake the inquiry.'[5] Thus, experiments are occasionally of no use; and at times, perhaps, 'instead of attempting to enquire after the cause [of something], which has hitherto been

[1] *Works* 5. 144-145.
[2] 4. 353.
[3] 1. 316.
[4] 1. 238.
[5] 1. 236.

inscrutable, it will best become us to rest satisfied with admiration; '[1] for 'the true end of studying Nature is to make a just selection, to find those parts of it that most conduce to our pleasure or convenience, and to leave the rest in neglect.'[2] 'To be well acquainted with the appearances of Nature, even though we are ignorant of their causes, often constitutes the most useful wisdom.'[3]

This last manner of studying nature, however, Goldsmith would call the one proper, not to experimental philosophy, but to natural history. As we have already seen from his preface, he felt that, though we dignify natural history 'never so much with the grave appellation of *a useful science*, yet we still must confess that it is the occupation of the idle and speculative, more than of the busy and the ambitious part of mankind.' Therefore, 'while the merchant and the mariner are solicitous in describing currents and soundings, the naturalist is employed in observing wonders, though not so beneficial, yet to him of a much more important nature.'[4] Since, then, Goldsmith considers the study of natural history as mere amusement, or, at most, as instructive amusement, it is not to be wondered at that he seems to hold a brief against such writers as make natural history dull and uninteresting to any but an expert. He recognizes, nevertheless, the great value of system in scientific study, and states the matter in very definite terms:[5]

> Method . . . is one of the principal helps in natural history, and without it very little progress can be made in this science.

[1] 1. 281.
[2] 2. 292.
[3] 1. 396.
[4] 1. 233.
[5] 2. 289-290.

It is by that alone we can hope to dissipate that glare, if I may so express it, that arises from a multiplicity of objects at once presenting themselves to the view. It is method that fixes the attention to one point, and leads it, by slow and certain degrees, to leave no part of Nature unobserved. . . .

These methodical divisions some have treated with contempt,[1] not considering that books, in general, are written with opposite views : some to be read, and some only to be occasionally consulted. The methodists, in natural history, seem to be content with the latter advantage ; and have sacrificed to order alone, all the delights of the subject, all the arts of heightening, awakening, or continuing curiosity. But they certainly have the same use in science that a dictionary has in language ; but with this difference, that in a dictionary we proceed from the name to the definition ; in a system of natural history, we proceed from the definition to find out the thing. Without the aid of System, Nature must still have lain undistinguished, like furniture in a lumber-room ; every thing we wish for is there, indeed ; but we know not where to find it.

In determining his own classification of quadrupeds, Goldsmith says :

We see, from this sketch of division and subdivision, how a subject, extremely delightful and amusing in itself, may be darkened, and rendered disgusting. But, notwithstanding, Ray seems to be one of the most simple distributors ; and his method is still, and not without reason, adopted by many. Such as have been at the trouble to learn this method, will certainly find it useful ; nor would we be thought, in the least, to take from its merits ; all we contend for is, that the same information may be obtained by a pleasanter and an easier method.[2]

Scientific nomenclature seems to him likewise unnecessarily difficult :

These [long Greek] names, which mean no great matter when they are explained, may serve to guide in the furnishing of a cabinet ; but they are of very little service in furnishing the page of instructive history.[3]

[1] Mr. Buffon in his Introduction, &c.   GOLDSMITH.
[2] 2. 296.
[3] 1. 47.

De Seve delin.

C. Baquoy sculp.

LE ZEBRE.

Buffon's *Histoire Naturelle* 12. 20

Moreover, this zeal for systematic division and the multiplication of names often leads the scientists to neglect more fruitful study :

> When an animal [the musk animal] with which we are so nearly connected [Goldsmith merely means because we utilize its scent], is so utterly unknown, how little must we know of many that are more remote and unserviceable ! Yet naturalists proceed in the same train, enlarging their catalogues and their names, without endeavoring to find out the nature, and fix the precise history of those with which we are very partially acquainted. It is the spirit of the scholars of the present age, to be fonder of increasing the bulk of our knowledge than its utility; of extending their conquests, than of improving their empire.[1]

This attitude of Goldsmith toward science in general, and natural history in particular, must be kept in mind in considering his scientific sources, of which I am about to give a brief account. Linnæus, Ray, Willughby, and the rest, provide him more or less with a framework and with multitudinous details ; but for the elements which make *Animated Nature* amusing as well as instructive, we must look elsewhere.

Excluding Buffon, since his book is a work of mixed *genre*, we find that Goldsmith's principal scientific sources were Gesner, Swammerdam, Willughby, Ray, Brisson, Linnæus, and Réaumur, with a number of others of less importance. He mentions Aldrovandus again and again, but I do not believe he knew him directly. Aldrovandus' successors continually quote him, so that Goldsmith could have gathered all his knowledge of him from them ; and it is ever Goldsmith's practice to attain his ends with the least effort.

The earliest of these modern sources is Konrad von Gesner's *Historia Animalium*, the first volume of which

[1] 3. 89.

appeared at Zurich in 1556, and was soon followed by
three others. The final volume, dealing with reptiles,
was not published until 1587. The whole work makes
up a complete natural history, and has been called
the starting point of modern zoölogy. Gesner is best
known as a botanist, however, and published works
on various other subjects.[1] Goldsmith certainly knew
the *Historia Animalium*, though he naturally does not
follow it directly whenever later writers, having adopted
Gesner's system, provide him with a more convenient
guide.

One of the two main sources for Goldsmith's account
of insects is Jan Swammerdam's *Historia Generalis*.
Goldsmith gives a lively account of this philosopher:

> To Reaumur we are obliged for examining the manners of
> some with accuracy; but to Swammerdam for more. [Gold-
> smith speaks here of shell-fish, about which, as well as about
> insects these writers were authorities.] In fact, this Dutchman
> has lent an attention to those animals, that almost exceeds
> credibility: he has excelled even the insects he dissected, in
> patience, industry, and perseverance. It was in vain that this
> poor man's father dissuaded him from what the world con-
> sidered as a barren pursuit; it was in vain that an habitual
> disorder, brought on by his application, interrupted his efforts;
> it was in vain that mankind treated him with ridicule while
> living, as they suffered his works to remain long unprinted
> and neglected when dead: still the Dutch philosopher went
> on, peeping into unwholesome ditches, wading through fens,
> dissecting spiders, and enumerating the blood-vessels of a snail:
> like the bee, whose heart he could not only distinguish, but
> dissect, he seemed instinctively impelled by his ruling passion,
> although he found nothing but ingratitude from man, and
> though his industry was apparently becoming fatal to himself.[2]

[1] For example, *Mithridates de Differentibus Linguis*, an account
of about 130 known languages, with the Lord's Prayer in 22 tongues;
and his edition of the works of Ælian.

[2] 7. 17-18. See below, p. 76, for a bit of G.'s translation from
Swammerdam.

The title-page of the *Historia Generalis* is self-explanatory: JOHANNIS SWAMMERDAMII, Amstelædamensis, Doctoris Medici, HISTORIA INSECTORUM GENERALIS, in qua quæcunque ad INSECTA eorumque *mutationes* spectant, dilucide ex sanioris philosophiæ & experientiæ principiis explicantur, *etc.*, 1685. The book was written in Dutch, but Goldsmith used the Latin translation whose title I have quoted. The work is concise, and seems really to be set forth ' dilucide ex sanioris philosophiæ principiis.' It is not sprightly reading, however, and a short extract will serve to illustrate the sort of thing Goldsmith is thinking of when he objects to the dry systematizing of natural history:

IV. *Apes feræ*, sylvicolæ, campisque & hortis etiam familiares. Harum nobis *sex* sunt species, quarum una longissimis antennis est prædita ; altera corpore quasi serino atque piloso ; alia Vespas forma sua æmulatur.

V. *Apes Sylvestres Aldrovandi*, quæ *Moufeto* est *Vespa Solitaria*, a nobis ad hunc ordinem referuntur. Earum nobis est *nympha, vermiculi tela*, ipsum denique *Insectum* ; *niduli* ex lapillis, arenulis & glebulis contecti. . . .

Huc etiam referri deberent Goedarti *Apes mansuetæ*, si modo *Apes*, & non essent verius *muscæ* Quarto Mutationis ordini a nobis accensendæ.[1]

Nevertheless, the book is soundly scientific, and helped to make possible the work of Réaumur, Goldsmith's most important source for the history of insects.

Of René Antoine Ferchault de Réaumur, Cuvier says :

L'auteur a porté au plus haut degré la sagacité dans l'observation et dans la découverte de tous ces instincts si compliqués et si constans dans chaque espèce que maintiennent ces foibles créatures. Il pique sans cesse la curiosité par des détails nouveaux et singuliers, il est partout de la vérité la plus rigoureuse, et se fait lire avec l'intérêt le plus attachant.

[1] *Hist. Gen.*, p. 94.

This is exactly the sort of writer Goldsmith delights to follow, as we shall see later in the case of Buffon. Réaumur's *Mémoires pour Servir à l'Histoire des Insectes* appeared in six volumes, from 1734 to 1742, exactly uniform with the *Histoire Naturelle* of Buffon, which was to follow fifteen years later. It attempts to cover the whole field of true insects. It seems strange to us in this age of the deification of science that Réaumur should feel it necessary to justify his work, but so he does :

> Il en a même [des gens] qui regardent toutes les connoissances de cette partie de l'Histoire Naturelle comme inutiles, qui les traitent, sans hésiter, d'amusements frivoles. Nous voulons bien aussi qu'on les regarde comme amusements, c'est-à-dire, comme des connoissances qui, loin de peiner, occupent agréablement l'esprit qui les acquiert ; elles font plus, elles l'élèvent nécessairement à admirer l'auteur de tant de prodigues. Devons-nous rougir de mettre même au nombre de nos occupations, les observations & les recherches qui ont pour objet des ouvrages où l'Estre suprême semble s'être plû à renfermer tant de merveilles, & les varier si fort ? L'Histoire Naturelle est l'histoire de ses ouvrages, il n'est point de démonstration de son existence, plus à la portée de tout le monde que celles qu'elles nous fournit.[1]

Goldsmith used this work continually, and particularly in considering bees. This leads me to think that he may have known also a translation of the part of the *Mémoires* dealing with those insects, which was published in 1744. I have not seen this book, however, and so can not offer an opinion. It will be noticed, when I treat in the next chapter of Goldsmith's method, that Goldsmith is himself not quite free of the cast of mind which Réaumur is combating in the passage just quoted.

For much of the history of birds, Goldsmith went directly to the *Ornithology* of Francis Willughby,[2] ' the

---

[1] *Mémoires* i. 3-4.

[2] Goldsmith spells his name ' Willoughby '.

first naturalist who treated the study of birds as a science, and the first who made anything like a rational classification.' It was, in fact, upon Willughby's system that Linnæus founded his ornithological classification. The *Ornithology* was first published in Latin, with revisions by John Ray, but the edition Goldsmith knew was the English version, also by Ray, which appeared in 1678. Between Willughby and Ray existed a most interesting and productive friendship. The two men traveled and studied together; and Ray published his friend's *Historia Piscium* (1686) and *Methodus Insectorum* (1705, appearing a short time after Ray's own death). Ray's posthumous *Historia Insectorum* (1710) also is full of acknowledgements to Willughby. The *Ornithology* is in many respects a remarkable book. It is a large folio, beautifully printed, and couched in a most lively, if not always rhetorically correct, English. The plates are perhaps a little stiff, but they are as trustworthy as Willughby and Ray could contrive to have them.[1] The volume includes not only an ornithology,

[1] Cf. Ray's Preface: ' Now because elegant and accurate Figures do much illustrate and facilitate the understanding of Descriptions, in order to the Engraving such Figures for this work, Mr. *Willughby* made a collection of as many Pictures drawn in colours by the life as he could procure. First, he published of one *Leonard Baltner*, a Fisherman of *Strasburgh*, a Volume containing the Pictures of all the Water-fowl frequenting the *Rhene* near that City, as also all the Fish and Water-Insects found there, drawn with great curiosity and exactness by an excellent hand. The which Fowl, Fishes, and Insects the said *Baltner* had himself taken, described, and at his own proper costs and charges caused to be drawn. Which curiosity is much to be admired and commended in a Person of his Condition and Education. For my part, I must needs acknowledge that I have received much light and information from the Work of this poor man, and have been thereby inabled to clear many difficulties and rectify some mistakes in *Gesner*. . . . Besides what he left, the deservedly famous Sir *Thomas Brown*, Professor

c

but treatises on fowling and on falconry as well—a
most spirited treatment, which clearly interested Goldsmith. The classification is logical and practical. First
Willughby notes two great classes, land- and water-
fowl ; the former are divided into rapacious birds, the
crow kind, the woodpecker kind, the poultry kind, the
pigeon kind, the thrush kind, and so on ; and the
water-fowl are similarly divided and subdivided. Goldsmith, following Linnæus, but undoubtedly having
Willughby's classification in mind, employs much the
same divisions. The revival of enthusiasm observable
in *Animated Nature* at the beginning of the history of
birds is, I think, in part due to the lively quality of
Willughby's book, as Ray presents it. Ray performed
his task as a labor both of love and of duty, as he shows
us in his Preface :

> Viewing his Manuscripts after his Death, I found the several
> Animals in every kind both Birds, Beasts, Fishes, and Insects
> digested into a Method of his own contriving, but few of their
> Descriptions and Histories so full and perfect as he intended
> them ; which he was so sensible of, that when I asked him upon
> his death-bed, whether it was his pleasure that they should be
> published, he answered, that he did not desire it, nor thought
> them so considerable as to deserve it, or somewhat to that
> purpose, for the very words I do not well remember, though

of Physick in the City of *Norwich*, frankly communicated the
Draughts of several rare Birds, with some brief notes and descriptions of them. . . .
 ' The Gravers we employed, though they were very good Work-
men, yet in many Sculps they have not satisfied me. For I being
at a great distance from *London*, and all advices and directions
necessarily passing by Letter, sometimes through haste mistook
my directions, sometimes through weariness and impatience of long
writing sent not so clear and full instructions as was requisite ; and
they as often neglected their instructions, or mistook my meaning.
Notwithstanding the Figures, such as they are, take them all together, they are the best and truest, that is, most like the live Birds,
of any hitherto engraven in Brass.'

he confessed there were in them some new and pretty observations about Insects. But, considering that the publication
of them might conduce somewhat 1. To the illustration of
Gods glory, by exciting men to take notice of, and admire
his infinite power and wisdom displaying themselves in the
Creation of so many *Species* of Animals; And 2. To the
assistance and ease of those who addict themselves to this
most pleasant, and no less useful part of Philosophy; And 3.
Also to the honour of our Nation, in making it appear that
no part of real knowledge is wholly balked and neglected by us,
(he not contradicting) I resolved to publish them, and first
took in hand the *Ornithology.*

Of Ray's own work, Goldsmith used the *Synopsis
Methodica Avium et Piscium,* published posthumously
in 1713. This book is frankly nothing but a *Synopsis,*
and so has none of the charm of the *Ornithology.*

But the chief source of Goldsmith's knowledge of
birds was the *Ornithologie* of Mathurin Jacques Brisson.
This work, uniform, like Réaumur's, with Buffon's
Histoire Naturelle, is in six volumes, published in 1760.
It is written in both Latin and French, printed in
parallel columns. Goldsmith used this book as the basis
of his treatment of birds, much as he employed Buffon
for the quadrupeds and Réaumur for the insects, although
Brisson is obtrusively, and perhaps excessively, systematic, and lacks the charm of style both Buffon and Réaumur possess. But he provided Goldsmith with a wealth
of fact and a great number of plates, which, with the
other material Goldsmith had to draw upon, was quite
sufficient to make the history of birds as attractive as
the rest of *Animated Nature.*

I might continue enumerating works of this sort;
but I trust that those already touched upon will give
an idea of the nature of Goldsmith's purely scientific
sources, and so, pausing only to mention a very important one, Linnæus, I refer the reader to the appendix
for the rest. Karl von Linné, or as he is better known

by his Latin name, Carolus Linnæus, is chiefly famous
as a botanist ; but he did invaluable work in the other
departments of natural history.   His great contribution
is classification, and like all these early scientists who
were attempting to bring order out of chaos, he regarded
his work almost in the light of a religious duty.   At
the very beginning of his *Systema Naturæ* he quotes :
' Docuisti me DEUS a juventute mea, & usque nunc
pronunciabo Mirabilia Tua ;' and in his introduction
he goes on to say :

> *Finis* Creationis *telluris est gloria* DEI *ex opere* Naturæ *per*
> Hominem *solum*.
>
> Tanto igitur magis nosse Naturam operæ pretium, quo nullum
> majus est ! neque enim quidquam habet in se hujus materiæ
> tractatio pulchrius, cum multa lateant futura usui, quam
> quod nominem Magnificentia sua detinet, nec mercede, sed
> Miraculo colitur.[1]
>
> Quota enim pars operis Tanti nostris oculis committitur, &
> quam multa, præter hæc, quæ vidimus, in secretum sunt nun-
> quam humanis oculis orientia ; neque enim omnia DEUS hum-
> anis oculis nota fecit.   Multa etenim sunt quæ esse audivimus,
> qualia autem sint ignoramus ! quamque multa hoc primum
> cognivimus seculo ! & quidem multa venientis ævi populus,
> ignota nobis, sciet ! . . . veniet tempus, quo ista quæ nunc
> latent, in lucem dies extranat & longioris ævi diligentia.   Rerum
> enim Natura sacra sua non simul tradit ; initiatos nos credimus,
> in vestibulo ejus hæremus ; illa arcana non promiscue, non
> omnibus patent ! reducta & interiori sacrario clausa sunt ; in-
> voluta veritas in alto latet. . . .
>
> Intravi itaque densas umbrosasque Naturæ Silvas, hinc inde
> horrentes acutissimis & hamatis spinis, evitavi quotquot licuit
> plurimas, at neminem tam esse circumspectum didici, cujus
> non diligentia sibi ipsi aliquando excidat, ideoque ringentium
> Satyrorum cachinnos, humerisque insilientium similiorum
> speculationes sustinui, incessi viam & quem dederat cursum
> fortuna peregi.[2]

[1] Goldsmith's exaltation of *wonder* reflects this idea.
[2] It is curious to note how the style of these writers combines
the tone of the Vulgate with that of the classic writers.   This

Linnæus' work in general, however, is pure cataloguing. Goldsmith certainly knew the *Systema Natura per Regna Tria* (Leyden, 1735, with many later and augmented editions), and the *Animalium Specierum . . . Methodica Dispositio* (1759) which completed the *Systema*. In addition to these he knew, at least in part, the *Amœnitates Academicæ, seu Dissertationes Variæ Physicæ, Medicæ, Botanicæ,* etc. (10 volumes, 1749), which he may have used in his medical studies. I shall have occasion to speak in the next chapter of his use of these classifications of Linnæus.

But of all the works Goldsmith used, Buffon's *Histoire Naturelle* is by far the most important. It is almost impossible to overestimate the influence of this book upon the first four volumes of *Animated Nature*. There is scarce a page without a bit of translation, or a fact, or a stolen reference, or some fainter reminiscence of the French work. And more than that, the *Histoire Naturelle* is responsible in a great measure, not merely for the principal inspiration and much of the plan of the whole work, but also for the very manner and tone. Goldsmith has the knack of adopting a suggestion and making it, at least apparently, quite his own. Hence, his attitude toward science in general, and natural history in particular, has, as I have indicated it, a flavor of original thinking; but I have found by more than one disappointing experience that many of his apparently most characteristic utterances have very definite sources, and, as often as not, are little more than translations. In this study, therefore, I do not present an idea as Goldsmith's own unless it is supported by seve-

same introduction quotes Seneca in the body of it, and concludes with a quotation from the Psalms: ' O Jehova ! Quam magnifica sunt Tua Opera ! Vir insipiens non cognoscit ea & stultus non animadvertit ea.'

ral passages ; for otherwise it may very easily have been
taken over bodily from some other work. Buffon has
provided innumerable aphorisms of this sort, though I
make no pretense of having even tried to trace them all.

The *Histoire Naturelle, Générale et Particulière, avec
la Description du Cabinet du Roy,* addressed to the king
by ' les très-humbles, très-obéissans & très-fidèles sujets
& serviteurs, Buffon, Intendant de votre Jardin des
Plantes,' and ' Daubenton, Garde & Démonstrateur de
votre Cabinet d'Histoire Naturelle,' began to be published
at Paris in 1749, but the fifteenth volume—the last in
the history of quadrupeds—did not appear until 1767.
The two first volumes of the history of birds appeared
in 1770 and 1773 respectively. Goldsmith allows us
to infer that he knew nothing beyond the volumes on
quadrupeds ; [1] but it is certain, both from textual evidence, and from evidence of a different sort which I shall
present later, that he knew at least the first volume
on birds. His descriptions of the ostrich and the dodo,
for example, compared with Buffon's give positive proof
of this. He did not, however, know the second volume.
One other matter has come up in connection with the
matter of editions, for which I have yet found no adequate explanation. At 4. 247, for example, we find
the footnote: ' Buffon, vol. xxi. p. 212,' but the place
in the first edition of Buffon where the animal in question
—the marmose—is discussed is in volume ten, and I
know of no edition Goldsmith might have used which
more than doubles the number of volumes of the original.
It could not have been a translation, because there was
none in Goldsmith's life-time. Nevertheless—for the
references are consistent—Goldsmith's edition of the
History of Quadrupeds was in at least thirty volumes,

---

[1] See the parts of his preface already quoted above, pp. 14-17.

and, as I shall show later, probably contained the original engravings. For the present, the matter must rest there.

The original edition of the *Histoire Naturelle* presents an appearance altogether befitting the royalty of its patron. It is in large quarto, bound in polished and gilded calf, which, in the set I have before me, has suffered little from time. The pages are rubricated on the edges, and are beautifully printed with two-inch margins, apparently with all the care the Imprimerie Royale could muster. *Animated Nature* itself at first sight is a bit imposing, but beside this aristocrat it shrinks to mediocrity. Not the least charm of the *Histoire Naturelle* lies in the exquisite engravings which crowd all the volumes after the two first. *Animated Nature*, too, is copiously illustrated; but, as I shall presently show, Goldsmith's plates, for more than one reason, are painfully poor beside those of the lordly *Histoire Naturelle*. It would be interesting to know whether Goldsmith owned the set of Buffon which he used, for it must have cost a pretty penny.

The whole credit of the *Histoire Naturelle* is popularly given to the Comte de Buffon, but no inconsiderable portion of it is due to Daubenton. Buffon, to be sure, is responsible for the *Théorie de la Terre* and *Preuves de la Théorie de la Terre* which fill the first volume, and, in the greater part, for the natural history of man and of animals in general that occupies the second. But from that point on through most of the volumes dealing with quadrupeds, Daubenton provides at least a third of the matter. Buffon is the nobleman with scientific leanings. With ruffles turned back, he does in person peer into the entrails of sheep or hare, but his expression is always ' je fis ouvrir un lapin,' or ' une vache,' or ' une chienne,' and never ' j'ouvris.'

Daubenton, however, seems more of the true scientist. It is he that provides the anatomical descriptions of the animals, gives tables of their measurements, and, no doubt, superintended the preparation of the anatomical plates. It is only where the particular quadrupeds are not at hand to dissect that he fades into the background. Nevertheless, I do not mean to disparage the work of Buffon himself; it is astounding, in this day of specialists, to think of a man to whom science was scarcely more than an avocation attempting a work of such scope, and executing it with such an apparent mastery of the minutest details. Besides this, it is Buffon that sets the tone of the work—a fact which Goldsmith perfectly realized; for, while he gives full credit to Daubenton when he borrows from him, he never acknowledges him as a source of inspiration.

The first volume of the *Histoire Naturelle* is entirely taken up by Buffon's general statement of his position in regard to the study of natural history, and with his theory of the formation of the earth. A consideration of the earth's form and substance Buffon thinks altogether essential to a complete natural history:

> Il n'est question ici ni de la figure de la Terre, ni de son mouvement, ni des rapports qu'elle peut avoir à l'extérieur avec les autres parties de l'Univers; c'est sa constitution intérieure, sa forme & sa matière que nous proposons d'examiner. L'histoire générale de la terre doit précéder celle de ses productions, & les détails des faits singuliers de la vie & les moeurs des animaux ou de la culture & la végétation des plantes appartiennent moins à l'Histoire Naturelle que les résultats généraux des observations qu'on a faites sur les différentes matières qui composent la globe terrestre, sur les éminences, les profondeurs & les inégalités de sa forme, sur le mouvement des mers, sur la direction des montagnes, sur la position des carrières, sur la rapidité & les effets des courants de la mer, &c. Ceci est la Nature en grand, & ce sont-là ses principales opérations, elles influent sur toutes les autres, & la théorie de

Headpiece to the second volume of Buffon's *Histoire Naturelle*

ces effets est une première science de laquelle dépend l'intelligence des phénomènes particuliers, aussi-bien que la connoissance exacte des substances terrestres; et quand même on voudroit donner à cette partie des sciences naturelles le nom de *Physique*, toute Physique où l'on n'admet point de systèmes n'est pas l'Histoire de la Nature.[1]

Accordingly, the learned count proceeds to take up the various theories proposed to account for the globe as we know it, and consider how they agree with his own, presenting in his so-called *Preuves* an immense amount of information concerning mountains, caverns, lakes, rivers, the ocean, volcanoes, earthquakes, winds, and other allied matters. Goldsmith follows the first volume a good deal in covering the same subjects, but, as his object is entertainment rather than argument, his treatment is naturally somewhat different. I shall discuss his handling of the matter in the next chapter.

Buffon's attitude toward the study of natural history is much the same as Goldsmith's, who, as I have said, received many of his general ideas about science from Buffon, except that Buffon inveighs even more strenuously against the over-systematizing of it. System-makers,

voulant tout ramener à leur point de vûe particulier, . . . se rétrécissent l'esprit, cessent de voir les objects tels qu'ils sont & finissent par embarrasser la science & la charger du poids étranger de toutes leurs idées.

On ne doit donc pas regarder les méthodes que les Auteurs nous ont données sur l'Histoire Naturelle en général, ou sur quelques-unes de ses parties, comme les fondemens de la science, & on ne doit s'en servir que comme de signe dont on est convenu pour s'entendre. . . . Chacune de ses méthodes n'est, à parler vrai, qu'un Dictionnaire où l'on trouve les noms rangés dans un ordre relatif à cette idée, & par conséquent aussi arbitraire que l'ordre alphabétique.[2]

---

[1] *Hist. Nat.* i. 65-66.
[2] *Hist. Nat.* i. 21-22.

But some sort of order is necessary if the study of nature is to take a convenient and useful form. The question is, what order is best:

> A l'égard de l'ordre général & de la méthode de distribution des différens sujets de l'Histoire Naturelle, on pourroit dire qu'il est purement arbitraire, & dès-lors on est assez le maître de choisir celui qu'on regarde comme le plus commode ou le plus communément reçu ; mais avant que de donner les raisons qui pourroient déterminer à adopter un ordre plûtôt qu'un autre, il est nécessaire de faire encore quelques réflexions, par les-quelles nous tâcherous de faire ce qu'il peut y avoir de réel dans les divisions que l'on a faites des productions naturelles[1].

These 'réflexions', if we consider how nature would appear to a man newly introduced into the world, will lead us to a natural arrangement. Such a man would first distinguish between inanimate matter and animate nature, and, soon after, between mobile living organisms and immobile. So we have the three primary divisions into mineral, animal, and vegetable. Next, he would at once perceive the further division into quadrupeds, birds, and fishes. Thus, by pursuing this rather naïve observation of the plan of nature, we arrive at not merely a coherent, but a truly natural system. Proceeding further, our hypothetical man would be first interested in those animals which most immediately concerned him, and only through his first observations of them would he turn his interest to those more remote. Thus Buffon arrives at his order of treatment:

> Cet ordre le plus naturel de tous, est celui que nous avons cru devoir suivre. Notre méthode de distribution n'est pas plus mystérieuse que ce qu'on vient de voir ; nous partons des divisions générales telles qu'on vient de les indiquer, & que personne ne peut contester, & ensuite nous prenons les objets qui nous intéressent le plus par les rapports qu'ils ont avec nous, & de-là nous passons peu à peu jusqu'à ceux qui sont

[1] *Hist. Nat.* i. 31.

les plus eloignés & qui sont étrangers, & nous croyons que cette
façon simple et naturelle de considérer les choses, est préférable
aux méthodes les plus recherchées & les plus composées, parce
qu'il n'y en a pas une, & de celles qui sont faites, et de toutes
celles que l'on peut faire, où il n'y ait plus d'arbitraire que dans
celle-ci, & qu'à tout prendre il nous est plus facile, plus agré-
able & plus utile de considérer les choses par rapport à nous,
que sous aucun autre point de vûe.

How far Goldsmith followed this same method I shall
discuss in the next chapter.

But, like all simple and logical analyses, this system
is easier to evolve than to put into consistent practice,
though it undoubtedly begins well. The second volume
starts with a general discussion of animals, which is
quite necessary, of course, though its proportion is
spoiled by a long and detailed account of Buffon's and
Daubenton's experiments upon the generation of animals,
and the development of their theory of the nature and
properties of the generative fluids. Then—still according
to the plan—comes the natural history of man himself;
and we find chapters on infancy, puberty, maturity, old
age, the senses, the varieties of mankind, and so on,
much of which Goldsmith puts into his book also. Then
follows the bulk of the work, the descriptions of individual kinds of quadrupeds. Here, too, at first, when
dealing with the domestic animals, the plan works out
rather neatly; but when the animals become more
difficult to relate to domestic counterparts, a somewhat chaotic arrangement—or lack of it—results, so that
Goldsmith is justified in saying that Buffon sets down
the animals almost as they happen to occur to him.
This lack of form does not, however, extend to the
individual descriptions. They begin usually with an
account of the animal's appearance, habitat, habits, and
so on, not forgetting its method of reproduction, in
which, as I have just said, Buffon had a particular in-

terest, and continue with a certain number of interesting details or illustrative anecdotes, which serve to lend color to the narrative. All this is by Buffon himself. Then follow, whenever the material is at hand, an account by Daubenton of the anatomy of the animal, and a description of that part of the king's collection which concerns it. This portion is always accompanied by very carefully and beautifully drawn plates. The whole combines both entertainment for the idle reader and extremely valuable information for the serious scientist.

The *Histoire Naturelle* is in a great measure responsible for the shape, and for at least a third of the substance, of *Animated Nature*.[1] From it Goldsmith borrows by direct and indirect quotation, and even by a sort of abbreviated quotation, which, when he mentions his source, as he usually does, is likely to misrepresent somewhat the original, and when he does not take the trouble to indicate whence it comes, is, to a modern eye at least, dangerously near plagiarism.[2] Nevertheless, there seems no real intent to deceive, since unacknowledged passages are in the original often right beside acknowledged ones, ready to be discovered by the first inquisitive reader that turns to Buffon. I have already spoken of Goldsmith's habit of appropriating references to writers he has never seen and perhaps never before heard of—a practice which certainly makes a modern scholar doubt his honesty; but the attitude of the eighteenth century toward the practice of quotation and citation seems to have lacked something of ethics, from

---

[1] Some striking examples of the influence of the *Histoire Naturelle* upon the engravings of *Animated Nature*, I reserve for the end of this chapter, in order not to confuse the discussion of the literary influences.

[2] Examples of these methods of borrowing will be found in the next chapter.

the present point of view. The matter of this attitude has never been adequately investigated, and would make a profitable study.[1]

But apart from these definite things, of which one can give concrete examples, Buffon's work had a more subtle effect on Goldsmith. The *Histoire Naturelle* was

[1] Two of Boswell's papers in *The Hypochondriack* essays (No. 21 and No. 22) are important in this connection—particularly the following extracts:

' We shall often find that Quotation is only an ostentatious display, or perhaps affection of learning. In the first case it is truly pedantry, and a fit subject for ridicule; in the latter it is imposition, and when detected deserves a more severe censure. Many authors quote only at second-hand by adopting Quotations inserted in the writings of other authors; or quote only from indexes, so that what they quote is probably all they have read of the books which they formally cite.' (*London Mag.*, June, 1779).

' I am about to offer some thoughts upon that sameness or similarity which we frequently find between passages in different authors without quotation. This may be one of three things; either what is called *Plagiarism*, or *Imitation*, or coincidence. . . . I must candidly acknowledge, that, in my opinion, the sameness or similarity which we frequently find between passages in different authors cannot be with absolute certainty ascribed to its proper origin unless where there is a passage of considerable length in one author, which we can discover in the very same words in another author; and then we may without hesitation pronounce that it is *Plagiarism*. . . . In Goldsmith's beautiful little poem, *The Hermit*, there is a delicate little philosophical sentiment:

" Man wants but little here below,
    Nor wants that little long,"

which is certainly borrowed from Dr. Young's *Night Thoughts*:

" Man wants but little, nor that little long."

Goldsmith, I suppose, had got the line by heart; and it had afterwards remained unperceived amongst his own store of poetical thoughts.' (*London Mag.*, July, 1779.)

Boswell is charitable; I am not so sure, from what I have seen in *Animated Nature*, that Goldsmith did not know perfectly well whence his ' delicate little philosophical sentiment ' came.

by far the most powerful single agent, excepting only
Goldsmith's own personality and literary style, in setting
the *tone* of *Animated Nature*. Buffon, speaking of his
plan, sets forth what he considers the attributes of a
proper natural history; and the description sounds as
if he had *Animated Nature* prophetically in mind, for
it fits Goldsmith's book even better than it does Buffon's :

> Ce plan général doit être suivi & rempli avec toute l'exacti-
> tude possible, & pour ne pas tomber dans une répétition trop
> fréquente du même ordre, pour éviter la monotonie du style,
> il faut varier la forme des descriptions & changer le fil de
> l'histoire, selon qu'on le jugera nécessaire; de même pour
> rendre les descriptions moins sèches, y mêler quelques faits,
> quelques comparaisons, quelques réflexions sur les usages des
> différentes parties, en un mot, faire en sorte qu'on puisse vous
> lire sans ennui aussi bien que sans contention.[1]

I am not sure that one can read *Animated Nature* altogether *sans contention*, but I am certain that there
is little excuse for *ennui*.

These books are the principal scientific sources of
Animated Nature; but they are by no means the only
ones Goldsmith mentions at first hand. Most of the
writers referred to in *Animated Nature* are mentioned
only once or twice, while some few are named again
and again. The first impulse, when one remembers the
unreliability of Goldsmith's references as indications of
his reading, is to discard as real sources such works
as are but rarely cited, and to accept all those to which
there is a considerable number of references. This
method, however, is faulty, for I have traced several
of the latter sort to Buffon, and have been forced to
acknowledge the authenticity of several that are mentioned only once. The nature of the reference is often
the only guide, unless Buffon or some other indubitable

[1] *Hist. Nat.* I. 31.

source proves that the citation could have come through it ; and even then the case is not closed, since Goldsmith may often have known the work which he cites, but, rather than spend time in looking for the passage himself, have used Buffon's reference, which his memory told him was correct. Nevertheless, I have constantly omitted such doubtful works from the list of sources set down in this study, as, indeed, I have passed over certain others, which, though I have not discovered where Goldsmith got the references, seem doubtful for some other reason. Hearsay may often account for such citations.[1]

The greatest number of names scattered through *Animated Nature* are those of travelers who, along with other information, have contributed facts of natural history. With comparatively few exceptions, these works seem to have come to Goldsmith's notice through Buffon, or one of the other principal sources. Usually his knowledge of them went no further ; but occasionally one is forced to believe that he had seen them at first hand. It is not to be supposed, however, that he possessed a large number of books of travel; rather I should conjecture that he used one or two of the fairly numerous compendiums of travel before the public in his day. One of these may have been an edition of Purchas ; one passage in particular—interesting because of an indubitable connection with Coleridge's *Ancient Mariner* [2]—apparently comes from Purchas, though Goldsmith's practice—which I shall treat more fully in the next chapter—of altering everything he quotes or borrows to bring it into harmony with his own style,

---

[1] See Appendix.

[2] Goldsmith's passage runs (1. 239-240) : ' Sir Robert Hawkins [*sic*; it was really *Richard* Hawkins], one of our most enlightened navigators, gives the following account of a calm . . . : '' Were it

makes it a little difficult to prove the fact. It is exceedingly probable that Goldsmith was familiar with
J. Newbery's collection of Travels, *The World Displayed;
or a Curious Collection of Voyages and Travels, selected
from Writers of all Nations.* . . . London, 1759. This
work was in twenty small volumes, and had an introduction written by Samuel Johnson.[1] Unfortunately
I have been able to see only one volume (the fourth)
of this book.   Other possible collections are : John
Harris' *Navigantium et Itinerantium Bibliotheca; or, a*

not," says he, " for the moving of the sea, by the force of winds,
tides, and currents, it would corrupt all the world.   The experiment
of this I saw in the year 1590, lying with a fleet about the islands
of Azores, almost six months ; the greatest part of which time we
were becalmed.   Upon which all the sea became so replenished
with several sorts of jellies, and forms of serpents, adders, and
snakes, as seemed wonderful ; some green, some black, some yellow,
some white, some of divers colours, and many of them had life ;
and some there were a yard and a half, and two yards long ; which
had I not seen, I could hardly have believed and hereof are witnesses all the company of the ships which were then present ; so
that hardly a man could draw a bucket of water clear of some
corruption. . . ." '
    The Purchas passage is as follows : ' The experience I saw in Anno
1590, lying with a Fleete of her Majesties Ships about the Ilands
of the Azores almost six moneths, the greater part of the time
we were becalmed : with which all the Sea became so replenished
with severall sorts of gellyes, and formes of Serpents, Adders, and
Snakes, some yellow, some white, some of divers colours, and
many of them had life, and some there were a yard and a halfe,
and two yards long ; which had I not seene, I could hardly have
beleeved.   And hereof are witnesses all the Companies of the
Shippes which were then present ; so that hardly a man could
draw a Bucket of water cleere of some corruption.' (Hakluyt Society
reprint of 1625 edition, 17. 76 ; i. e., Purchas, book 7, part 2, § 2.)
The Coleridge passage is noted without comment on p. 58 of
Bethune's edition of the Hawkins voyages, prepared for the Hakluyt
Society, 1847.
    [1] W. P. Courtney, *Bibliography of Johnson*, p. 98.

Compleat Collection of Voyages and Travels, consisting of above Four Hundred of the Most Authentic Writers (the first edition was in 1705, and there were two others in 1744–1748 and 1764) ; the Astley collection, *A new General Collection of Travels; consisting of the most Esteemed Relations, which have been hitherto published in any Language. . . .* London, 1745, 4 vols. (this fine work was authorized by royalty, and is said to have given birth to Prévost's *Collection Générale*) ; and *A Collection of Voyages and Travels, consisting of authentic writers in our own tongue, . . . and continued with others of note, that have published histories, voyages, . . . or discoveries relating to . . . Asia, Africa, America, Europe, or the Islands thereof, from the earliest account to the present time. . . . Compiled from the . . . Library of the late Earl of Oxford.* London, 1745. To determine exactly which one of these or similar works Goldsmith actually used would entail a very careful comparison of his text with each one of these collections in turn— a work which I have not attempted, both because not all of them were easily accessible and because the solution of the problem would not have materially improved this study.[1]

There are, besides, several individual travelers whom Goldsmith knew fairly well. He mentions a number of times Dampier, ' that rough seaman, who has added more to natural history than half the philosophers that went before him.' He knew also Adanson's *Histoire Naturelle de Sénégal* (Paris, 1757), translated in 1759, with notes by ' an English Gentleman, who resided some time in that country,' under the title of *A Voyage to Senegal, the Isle of Goree, and the River Gambia,*

---

[1] I have, however, not neglected to examine such as I could come upon.

and published by J. Nourse, the future publisher of *Animated Nature.* Jean Baptiste Labat's *Nouvelle Relation de l'Afrique Occidentale* (5 vols., Paris, 1728) provides him with many facts, though he perhaps knew the work through one of the collections I have mentioned. Most of Goldsmith's knowledge of South America is drawn from *A Voyage to South America; describing at large the Spanish Cities . . . etc., of that extensive Continent. By Don George Juan, and Don Antonio de Ulloa, both Captains of the Spanish Navy, Members of the Royal Societies of London and Berlin, and Corresponding Members of the Royal Academy at Paris* (London, 1758). Some of Goldsmith's most pleasing remarks— about mountains, for example, and about the llama— come from this work. One other work, too, deserves particular mention, David Crantz'[1] *History of Greenland; containing a Description of the Country and its Inhabitants; and particularly, a Relation of the Mission, carried on for above these Thirty Years by the Unitas Fratrum . . . in that country.* The English translation was published by Dodsley in 1767. From this book, a really fascinating account of the missionizing of Greenland, full of valuable information acquired at first hand, Goldsmith got many of his most vivid details of the geography and animal life of the polar .regions. He mentions also Paul Egede's *History of Greenland,* but either takes his reference from Crantz, or has confused Paul Egede with his brother, Hans Egede, whose *Description of Greenland* appeared in an English translation in 1745. Both Paul and Hans Egede were members of the Unitas Fratrum, and each was for a time Bishop of Greenland. I do not find any history written by Paul Egede, though Crantz (1. 116, and elsewhere)

---

[1] Spelled also ' Cranz,' ' Kranz,' and ' Krantz.'

mentions his ' continuation of the Greenland relation.' The catalogue of the Library of the British Museum does not list the book. And so I might name other books of like nature, but, for the sake of brevity, prefer to relegate them to the Appendix. One curious fact is worth noting, however: of the two writers who provided him with so much of the material for *The Citizen of the World*, Du Halde and Le Comte,[1] he mentions Le Comte only four times, and Du Halde not at all.

Finally, Goldsmith does not altogether neglect the other sources of information which, to a modern scientist, would seem the most important—observation and personal inquiry. He apparently lost no opportunity of questioning his friends and acquaintances upon various abstruse matters. He says he has made inquiry of painters regarding the normal shape of the nose and general facial perfection, as well as about the manner of emotional expression in the face and about the general study of physiognomy.[2] He has found out from a magistrate the number of those who die of famine in London.[3] From ' a very credible traveller ' he has learned certain facts concerning the great apes,[4] and has been ' assured, by many persons of credit, that monkeys can not be taken in traps.' [5] In regard to the race of giants reported to have been seen on Byron's voyage, he says: ' I have talked with ɟhe person who first gave the relation of that voyage,

---

[1] As proved by Hamilton Smith's unpublished Yale dissertation, *The Sources and Literary Relations of Goldsmith's Citizen of the World*. See below, p. 154.

[2] 2. 88, 91, 94.

[3] 2. 130.

[4] 4. 205.

[5] 4. 228.

and who was the carpenter of the Commodore's ship; he was a sensible, understanding man, and I believe extremely faithful. By him, therefore, I was assured, in the most solemn manner, of the truth of his relation; and this account has since been confirmed by one or two publications; in all which the particulars are pretty nearly the same.'[1] Thus, in spite of the myriad facts he sets down upon the unsupported authority of others, Goldsmith was not altogether devoid of the desire to verify the information he retailed. Particularly when a matter is connected with medicine, we find him sifting the evidence, and often adding his own opinion.

He did not go through the world with his eyes shut either, and is never slow to offer his own observation of any fact or phenomenon. His vivid pictures of mountains show that he remembered his own trip across the Alps. In opposition to the opinion that the sense of taste is destroyed on high mountains, he says: ' I have been one of many, who have ate a very savoury dinner on the Alps.'[2] And in speaking of sheep following the shepherd's pipe:

> Before I had seen them trained in this manner, I had no conception of those descriptions in the old pastoral poets, of the shepherd leading his flock from one country to another. As I had been used only to see these harmless creatures driven before their keepers, I supposed that all the rest was but invention: but in many parts of the Alps, and even some provinces of France, the shepherd and his pipe are still continued, with true antique simplicity. The flock is regularly penned every evening, to preserve them from the wolf; and the shepherd returns homeward at sun-set, with his sheep following him, and seemingly pleased with the sound of the pipe, which is blown with a reed, and resembles the chanter of the bag-pipe.[3]

[1] 2. 261.
[2] 1. 335.
[3] 3. 42.

At ' Schathausen ' [1] on the Rhine he saw the cataracts frozen clear across.　He has seen the current of a river stopped by a violent storm, so that it ' was left entirely dry for some hours, and fish were caught among the stones at the bottom.' [2]　He remembers, ' upon approaching the coast [of Holland], to have looked down upon it from the sea, as into a valley.' [3]　He has even seen a waterspout :　' They sometimes appear in the calmest weather at sea, of which I have been an eyewitness ; and, therefore, these are not caused by a whirlwind.' [4]　He speaks about his own feeling in regard to the toad—how, though he had no instinctive loathing for it, the example of others soon made him shrink from it, like every one else. [5]　Occasionally, though he does not call attention to the observation as his own, the heartfelt note of personal experience is unmistakable.　The following passage is eloquent of Goldsmith's unenviable experiences both at home and on the continent, as well as of the sanitary conditions of the time :

> The Bug is another of those nauseous insects that intrude upon the retreats of mankind ; and that often banish that sleep, which even sorrow and anxiety permitted to approach.　This, to many men, is, of all other insects, the most troublesome and obnoxious.　The night is usually the season when the wretched have rest from their labour ; but this seems the only season when the bug issues from its retreats, to make its depredations.　By day it lurks, like a robber, in the most secret parts of the bed ; takes the advantage of every chink and cranny, to make a secure lodgment ; and contrives its habitation with so much art, that scarce any industry can discover its retreat.

[1] I. 221, i. e., Schaffhausen ?

[2] I. 207.

[3] I. 276.

[4] I. 395.　His conclusion is faulty, of course.

[5] 7. 91-92.

It seems to avoid the light with great cunning; and even if
candles be kept burning, this formidable insect will not issue
from its hiding place. But when darkness promises security,
it then issues from every corner of the bed, drops from the
tester, crawls from behind the arras, and travels with great
assiduity to the unhappy patient, who vainly wishes for rest
and refreshment. It is generally vain to destroy one only, as
there are hundreds more to revenge their companion's fate;
so that the person who thus is subject to be bitten, remains
the whole night like a centinel upon duty, rather watching the
approach of fresh invaders, than inviting the pleasing approaches
of sleep. . . .

These are a part of the inconveniences that result from the
persecution of these odious insects: but happily for Great
Britain, they multiply less in these islands, than in any part
of the continent. In France and Italy the beds, particularly
in their inns, swarm with them; and every piece of furniture
seems to afford them a retreat. They grow larger also with
them than with us, and bite with more cruel appetite.[1]

Goldsmith's discussion of dogs and horses seems also
to come from first-hand knowledge, though of a pleasanter sort. We learn, too, that the squirrel ' has an
extremely sharp piercing note, which most usually
expresses pain; it has another, more like the purring of
a cat, which it employs when pleased; at least it appeared
so in that from whence I have taken a part of this
description.' This particular little creature seems to
have made a very agreeable impression upon our naturalist, whom we may imagine at the time not in the
best of spirits, for not only is the whole account full
of sympathetic details, but it concludes in this manner:
' In short, it is a pleasing pretty little domestic; and
its tricks and habitudes may serve to entertain a mind
unequal to stronger operations.'[2] He observed seals,
also, at first hand for he tells us that ' a gentleman

[1] 7. 281-282.
[2] 4. 32, 34.

whom I knew in Ireland, kept two of them, which he
had taken very young, in his house for ten years ; and
they appeared to have the marks of age at the time
I saw them, for they were grown grey about the muzzle ;
and it is probable that they did not live many years
longer.' [1] To judge from his references, he never missed
an exhibit of any kind that bore any relation to natural
history. He has seen a Tartar, albino negroes, and all
sorts of strange animals and monstrosities (although
unnatural creations did not please him, as he tells us
in his chapter on Monsters). He observes that the
zebra

> which is now in the Queen's managerie, at Buckingham-Gate,
> is even more vicious than the former ; and the keeper who
> shews it takes care to inform the spectators of its ungovernable
> nature. Upon my attempting to approach, it seemed quite
> terrified, and was preparing to kick, appearing as wild as if
> just caught, although taken extremely young, and used with
> the utmost indulgence.[2]

The animals at the Tower seem to have absorbed a great
deal of his attention. He saw a siagush there ' a few
years ago,' as well as lions, tigers, leopards, etc. He
judged the size and appearance of a cougar, as well
as he could through the bars ; he questioned the keeper
as to the habits of the animals. On seeing the keeper
play with an ounce, he owns he ' was not a little uneasy,
at first, for the man, when he put his hand through
the bars.' [3] In fact, he was pretty well informed concerning such animals as the Tower contained, and must
have had a glorious time visiting them, to judge from
the apparent pleasure he takes in relating his observations. Goldsmith, for all his undoubted literary ability,

[1] 4. 177.
[2] 2. 393. The ' former ' is a zebra described by Buffon.
[3] 3. 260.

never lost a certain childlike wonder at even the commonplaces of nature, which, though it cause us to laugh at him, nevertheless lends his writing a freshness and force that more sophisticated writers often lack. Hence his personal observations brighten his narrative not a little, and so become an important element in the whole.

There is one other relation between *Animated Nature* and its sources which has nothing to do with the text of the work, and yet which indicates certain things about Goldsmith's methods, and the methods of hackwork in general. As I have said, the book is profusely illustrated with engravings, particularly in the part dealing with the less familiar quadrupeds. The plates are unsigned, badly drawn, with practically no claim to any sort of artistic merit. The figures are wooden, standing in impossible attitudes, with faces ludicrously human in their unlikeness to animal physiognomy. Nevertheless, the spacing in many of the drawings is good, revealing real knowledge of the rules of pictorial composition. The only possible solution for such an apparent contradiction is that they are wretched copies of much better originals.

Fortunately, these originals are in most cases not far to seek. Buffon's book provided Goldsmith not only with matter, but with illustrations as well. The plates in the *Histoire Naturelle* are beautifully done, apparently with few exceptions drawn from life. The signatures are usually *De Sève* or *Buvée l'Amériquain*, the former more often executing the pictures of the living animal, and the latter the anatomical sketches and the mounted skeleton (represented on a pedestal in a formal landscape, or sometimes on the same pedestal in a howling wilderness), though occasionally the rôles are exchanged.

The ZEBRA

Animated Nature 2. 390

It is only when they are drawing animals they could never have seen that the figures lose the vivid quality remarkable in the drawings of domestic animals. I reproduce three of the Buffon plates in conjunction with the corresponding ones from *Animated Nature*, having chosen these particular illustrations, not for their beauty (nor, indeed, for their ugliness; *Animated Nature* can provide many more hideous examples), but because they show various details of the artist's method of copying.

Not all of the pictures were taken from Buffon, of course, since Buffon had only just passed beyond the quadrupeds. For the birds, after appropriating Buffon's Eagle, King of the Vultures, and Ostrich, the artist (by courtesy) went to Brisson for the rest. A number of the plates I have not been able to trace : the Dodo, for example, could not have come from either Buffon or Brisson, since neither of them ventures to picture it ; and that it comes from Willughby (*Ornith.*, plate 27) seems to me doubtful also, since Goldsmith's Dodo is really more lifelike than Willughby's—a feat which our artist seems to have achieved nowhere else. The comparatively few pictures of fishes and insects I have not traced, nor have I found the originals of the figures representing the different races of man.

The reversed position of the figures reveals that the plates in *Animated Nature* were engraved directly from the originals, by means of very poor tools, and without any effort at originality on the part of the engraver. The copies are slavish in the extreme, even to the details of landscape, and the formation of the clouds in the sky. Another striking thing is his combining of two plates into one. I have chosen the Zebra to illustrate this, because it is one of the better pictures in *Animated Nature*, and shows a rather successful combination. There are a number of others, however, which consist of two, or even three, figures from as many plates, placed merely side by side, or one above the other. The original landscape settings of all the plates whose source I know are, with one exception, present in the originals. The fearfully gaunt Cassowary (Brisson, *Ornith.* 5. 16 ; *A. N.* 5. 67) was apparently too bare even for our artist, and he used what practice he had gained from copying Buffon's plates to provide a clumsy background for it ; but this is the only example in the book of his showing the least imagination. The other birds, and the fishes and insects, have to be content with a white ground.

In the presence of these examples, it is needless to say much about the artist's manner. One can not fail to notice how he has turned the delicate shading of the French engravings into a monotony of black and white ; though he was artist and engraver in one, he was not very good in either capacity. But a careful examination of the illustrations in the various eighteenth-century books on natural history which I have had to consider, and particularly those in the *Histoire Naturelle*, points the way to a most profitable study, which, though it has no part in the present one, I can not forbear mentioning briefly. All Buffon's pictures represent the animals in what the artists considered appropriate settings. Domestic animals are frequently pictured in surroundings that remind one of Dutch *genre* paintings ; the Great Dane, however, and other such aristocratic creatures are placed on marble terraces, with architectural palaces in the background, and, as often as not, distinctly naturalistic or romantic foliage in the immediate foreground. One dog, at least, stands against a moonlit, half-clouded sky, with what looks like a romantic castle off in one corner. The wild animals are, of course, shown in a more sylvan setting, revealing, from the care with which flowers and foliage are drawn, a desire for realism on the part of the artist. If the creature inhabits Egypt, there are pyramids or palm trees; if deserted solitudes, a fallen column or a ruined temple provides the proper atmosphere. China, when necessary, is very easily typified by a pagoda. The orang-outang was an object of great interest to an age which, while it dared not admit the great ape's affinity with man, yet was interested, if only to the point of amusement, by Monboddo, who believed that all men had once had tails which they had lost by the attrition of an habitual sedentary posture. Consequently it is not an insignificant fact that Buffon's orang-outang [1] is represented standing in close proximity to the haunts of men, and bearing a staff in an indubitably human manner.[2] In short, an extended study of such pictures would provide an additional key to our understanding of the philosophic, literary, and artistic thought of the eighteenth century. I am aware that this has been more than once attempted in connection with the more orthodoxly artistic field of landscape painting; but such pictures as these of Buffon have the advantage, for our purpose, of being intended for a public not primarily interested in art, and therefore of being closer to the popular mind, and illustrative less of a

---

[1] *H. N.* 14. 82; *A. N.* 4. 189. Buffon gives the name *Jocko* to this picture, and describes the jocko as a smaller ape which he believes is of the same species as the orang-outang. Strictly speaking, then, we must consider Goldsmith's label as a misnomer.

[2] Professor Tinker, who notes this picture in his *Nature's Simple Plan* (1922), apparently considers that the huts in the background belong to the animal itself. Since this point can be settled only by conjuring up the artist to explain his picture, I leave the matter here.

particular artist's theories than of the contemporary public taste.

But let us return to a phase of the question more nearly connected with *Animated Nature*. The only lettering upon the plates in Goldsmith's book, besides the title, is the numbering at the top, indicated in my illustrations. The first noticeable thing about this is that no single plate is at present inserted in the place corresponding to its marking. This alone is not remarkable—some of Buffon's plates are also misplaced; but the next fact is more significant. With only a few exceptions is any plate wrongly placed with reference to the text. At this point one might conclude that they were simply taken from other books, and that the marking referred to the original volume. However, if we tabulate these numberings, and compare them with the order in which the plates stand in *Animated Nature*, we are at once struck with the fact that in practically every case the order of treatment in *Animated Nature* and the order in which the plates were apparently intended to stand are *identical*.[1] Now comes a discrepancy: the work for which the plates were designed obviously was meant to be in only four volumes, though we know that *Animated Nature* was contracted for, paid for, and published in eight volumes. Does this mean that at some time during the preparation of the work, it was planned to reduce the book to four volumes, or does it mean that the pictures were taken from some other work whose plan of treatment was identical with that of *Animated Nature*? The former is possible, though hardly probable; the latter is flatly contradicted by Goldsmith's repeated assertions

---

[1] This fact will be more readily grasped from a table which I give in the Appendix, below, p. 151-152.

that, while in many places he follows for a time the system of some other writer, he himself is responsible for the arrangement as a whole. However, we must consider the possibility of the existence of such a work. If it existed, this hypothetical natural history consisted of four volumes of about four hundred pages apiece— about the size of the volumes of *Animated Nature*. It evidently followed Buffon just as closely as Goldsmith did, though certainly in less space. The proportion of the various parts was also about the same. The first volume apparently dealt with the earth and man; quadrupeds did not appear before volume 2, and continued at least through volume 3, page 26. The first bird picture was at volume 3, page 61, and so on, as shown in my table. Since certain pictures from Buffon's first volume on birds are used, the date of this imaginary history could not be earlier than 1770. I have not been able to find any such work; but if it exists, there is but one conclusion: Goldsmith is lying when he assumes the credit of originating the arrangement of his book; nevertheless, with all his faults, I have never found him making a deliberately false statement, and so am inclined to believe that there is some less harsh explanation of the matter. I present the evidence, therefore, for what it is worth, and can only hope that further investigation will solve the problem.

The examination of this question of the sources of *Animated Nature* shows indubitably that, however little original work there may be in it, we are not dealing with a *mere* compilation. Goldsmith has gone, at least, to the·proper places for his material. There was no better authority than Linnæus, and no pleasanter book on natural history than the *Histoire Naturelle*. Even in the matter of illustrations, only the fact that the artist was such a poor one kept the plates from being very fine : photography itself could scarcely exceed the realism of many of Buffon's pictures, and could certainly not improve upon the delicacy and softness of shading that we find in these engravings. In the next chapter, therefore, I shall consider how far Goldsmith has succeeded in shaping his excellent, but exceedingly heterogeneous, material into an harmonious whole.

CHAPTER III

GOLDSMITH'S METHOD AND MANNER IN
ANIMATED NATURE

In this chapter I propose to discover, if possible, in what Goldsmith's 'art of compiling' consisted. *Animated Nature* is a good compilation. It contains exceedingly few misstatements, beyond such as are due not to Goldsmith's error, but to the general condition of contemporary scientific knowledge; and it affords, besides, remarkably entertaining reading, as any one who knows it must testify. I was delighted with it at the first reading, and have never since been bored by it. Chance felicity of composition will not account for this in so long a work; it can only be the effect of art. Indeed, Goldsmith himself a short time before his death told Cradock: 'I never took more pains than in the first volume of my "Natural History"; surely that was good, and I was handsomely repaid for the whole. My Roman History, Johnson says, is well abridged.' [1] This first volume is, indeed, a beautiful piece of work, a literary entity in itself; but the whole history, though perhaps not so well polished in all its details, is just as well planned and proportioned, a fine example of 'the art of writing, which is but another name for good sense.' Herein lies one of the peculiar virtues of the book—an inherent literary form, which I have found to such a striking degree in none of its sources, not even in Buffon's *Histoire Naturelle*.

[1] Cradock, *Memoirs* 4. 281.

An examination of Goldsmith's plan in *Animated Nature* reveals a trait of which his biographers have failed to take adequate account—a remarkably keen judgment, the ability to decide among a number of conflicting opinions, and thus to produce an apparent simplicity in the midst of undoubted complexity. The first evidence we find of this is his ever-present consciousness of the fact that he is writing a popular treatise, and not a technically scientific one. Buffon may go at great length into the question of animal generation or embryology, or Daubenton, in the same work, may present a variety of information drawn from dissections or preserved specimens; Goldsmith refuses to let himself wander very far into these regions—though such matter might have added a greater air of learning to his book, and was just as easily come by as much of his other information. He seldom fails to note any interesting medical fact that comes up in connection with the animals he is discussing, but almost always stops before he reaches the point of carrying unmedical readers out of their depth—and yet in many cases he must have possessed further knowledge on the subject. Everywhere in the book one feels that Goldsmith's judgment is on the alert—here, perhaps, objecting to the theories that he has encountered respecting the cause of waterspouts, because he has seen some that can not be so accounted for, or elsewhere simply exerting itself to free the unfortunate porcupine from the charge of offensively shooting its quills; [1] thus, again, he repudiates reports of the crocodile's unmaternal conduct, since he feels that the crocodile is probably ' not more divested of parental tenderness than other creatures.' [2]

The first volume is, of course, based upon the first

[1] 4. 109-110.
[2] 7. 137.

volume of the *Histoire Naturelle*; but Goldsmith's purpose is quite different from Buffon's, and his finished volume is correspondingly unlike the French work. Buffon is mainly interested in establishing his theory of the earth, in opposition to various conflicting theories; details of the earth's structure and appearance are frankly adduced in corroboration of the theory. Goldsmith's purpose, on the other hand, is to give a comprehensive view of the earth and the various phenomena of inanimate nature. Consequently, Buffon's treatment requires much modification and amplification, for a certain knowledge of physics—which Buffon takes for granted in his reader—is necessary to the proper understanding of such phenomena. Accordingly, Goldsmith supplies this elementary knowledge, inserting it just at the proper place, and entirely rearranges Buffon's order of treatment, even when he makes little change in the matter itself. The table of contents of the first volume is worth quoting, because it shows how logically Goldsmith has arranged his matter, so that one chapter leads into another, and the whole volume becomes a progression from a consideration of the palpable globe itself to that of the phenomena of the atmosphere, terminating in a fine characteristic conclusion:[1]

[1] The italics are mine, and indicate chapters without counterparts in Buffon, though sometimes material from Buffon is used in them.

[2] This chapter is Goldsmith's own, though the subject is covered by Buffon's chapter, *Géographie*.

[3] Goldsmith follows Buffon somewhat here—though he probably knows the works in question—and proceeds to criticize Buffon's theory as well.

So we find that, out of twenty-two chapters, Goldsmith has written ten without the assistance of the *Histoire Naturelle*. This fact alone is enough to vindicate him from the charge of slavish imitation.

In the second volume, where he treats the natural history of animals in general, and of man in particular, Goldsmith follows Buffon rather closely, admittedly translating some chapters direct—though, as I shall soon show, 'translation,' in Goldsmith's sense, may mean not only free rendering, but also condensation.

[1] Goldsmith knew something of this subject. He used Hill's *Fossils* in preparing *Animated Nature*, and in a letter to Nourse, Feb. 1774, says: ' I have thoughts of extending the work into the *vegetable* and *fossil* kingdoms.'

[2] This chapter is only very partially covered by Buffon.

There is, however, even in this part, some interesting original writing, such, for example, as the chapter on sleep and hunger, and the essay on music inserted in the chapter on hearing, one of the chapters which Goldsmith's foot-note tells us is translated. Toward the end of the volume, however, we find two chapters exceedingly important to a discussion of Goldsmith's method —Chapter XIV, *Of Animals*,[1] and Chapter XV, *Of Quadrupedes in general, compared to Man*.[2] In the former he states his reasons for arranging the descriptions as he does, and in the latter gives a lively and highly colored panorama of the world of quadrupeds, where terror vies with terror, and where we are reassured concerning the wisdom of the whole scheme only by the demonstration that ' Providence has most wisely balanced the strength of the great against the weakness of the little. Since it was necessary that some should be great and others mean, since it was expedient that some should live upon others, it has assisted the weakness of one by granting it fruitfulness; and diminished the number of the other by infecundity.'[3] I shall return to this matter in my next chapter, but for the present must continue with Goldsmith's method.

The first paragraph of Chapter XIV illustrates perfectly Goldsmith's attitude toward the problem of scientific classification, which he had already partially stated in the preface :

> Leaving man, we now descend to the lower ranks of Animated Nature, and prepare to examine the life, manners, and characters of these our humble partners in the creation. But, in such a wonderful variety as is diffused around us, where shall we begin ! The number of beings, endued with life as well as

[1] 2. 288 ff.
[2] 2. 269 ff.
[3] 2. 335.

we, seems, at first view, infinite. Not only the forest, the waters, the air, teems [*sic*] with animals of various kinds; but almost every vegetable, every leaf, has millions of minute inhabitants, each of which fill [*sic*] up the circle of its allotted life, and some of which are found objects of the greatest curiosity. In this seeming exuberance of animals, it is natural enough for ignorance to lie down in hopeless uncertainty, and to declare what requires labour to particularize to be utterly inscrutable. It is otherwise however with the active and searching mind; no way intimidated with the immense variety, it begins the task of numbering, grouping, and classing all the various kind that fall within its notice; finds every day new relations between the several parts of the creation, acquires the art of considering several at a time under one point of view; and, at last, begins to find that the variety is neither so great nor so inscrutable as was at first imagined. As in a clear night, the number of stars seems infinite; yet, if we sedulously attend to each in its place, and regularly class them, they will soon be found to diminish, and come within a very scanty computation.[1]

Method must be used, therefore, but must be discarded wherever it becomes a hindrance rather than a help:

All method is only useful in giving perspicuity, where the subject is either dark or copious: but with regard to quadrupeds, the number is but few; many of them we are well acquainted with by habit; and the rest may very readily be known, without any method.[2]

Thus, though Goldsmith appears quite conversant with the books setting forth the various systems, and recommends that ' no inquirer in Nature should be without one of them; and without any doubt, Linnæus deserves the preference,' yet he considers that they do not really add to our knowledge:

Setting aside the impossibility of getting through whole volumes of a dry long catalogue, the multiplicity of whose con-

---

[1] 2. 288.   This belittling of the infinity of nature seems to me characteristic of eighteenth-century rationalism.
[2] 2. 293.

tents is too great for even the strongest memory; such works rather tell us the names than the history of the creature we desire to inquire after. In these dreary pages, every insect, or plant, that has a name, makes as distinguished a figure as the most wonderful, or the most useful.[1] The true end of studying Nature is to make a just selection, to find those parts of it that most conduce to our pleasure or convenience, and to leave the rest in neglect.[2]

Accordingly, Goldsmith decides to follow Buffon in essence, but to carry this ' common-sense ' classification even further than the French philosopher does. He therefore divides all quadrupeds into fourteen classes, as follows : [3] the Horse Kind, the Cow Kind, the Sheep Kind, the Deer Kind, the Hog Kind, the Cat Kind, the Dog Kind, the Weasel Kind, the Rabbit Kind, the Hedgehog Kind, the Tortoise Kind, the Otter Kind, the Ape and Monkey Kinds, and the Bat Kind. The principal advantage of this plan over Buffon's is that Goldsmith is enabled to draw together both domestic and wild varieties of the same animal, while Buffon usually separates them. Such obviously similar animals as the horse and the zebra are in Buffon placed nine volumes apart, whereas in *Animated Nature* they are given in the same class. Nevertheless, we can realize how unscientific this arrangement is when we notice that Goldsmith includes the flying-squirrel among the Bat Kind. There are, moreover, thirteen animals that refuse to fit into this system. ' The Elephant, the Rhinoceros, the Hippopotamus, the Camelopard (Giraffe), the Camel, the Bear, the Badger, the Tapir, the Cabiai,

---

[1] However unfair Goldsmith may be in this criticism, he is quite right in saying that books like Linnæus' *Systema* do exhibit a curious lack of emphasis.

[2] 2. 292.

[3] There is a certain reflection in this of Willughby's classification of birds, where we find this same sort of division into ' kinds.'

the Coati, the Antbear, the Tatou, and lastly the Sloth,'
' seem to approach no other kind, either in nature, or
in form, but to make each a distinct species in itself.'
However, it is no great matter if an animal is classed
under one head when it might better have been put
under another ; for ' all methods of this kind are merely
arbitrary, and . . . Nature makes no exact distinctions
between her productions. . . . To know them with any
precision, no system, or even description will serve,
since the animal itself, or a good print of it, must be
seen, and its history be read at length, before it can
be said to be known.' In the same clear way Goldsmith
threads his path among the difficulties in classifying
the other divisions of animals, not always, perhaps,
with the best feeling for scientific accuracy—as, for
example, when he insists, in the face of existing classifications, upon calling the whale a fish, but always
with the intention of simplifying the problem, and
choosing the most obvious order. And it must be confessed that, however pernicious this may be from the
point of view of exact science, in *Animated Nature*—
a book designed to present a panorama of the animal
world to readers who presumably know little or nothing
about it—the result is a clear and connected treatment.

But coherence does not come merely from a perfect
system, as the old lady discovered when she read the
dictionary, and pronounced it ' interesting, but dis-
connected.' Goldsmith is continually careful to mark
his transitions, and so group his material that the reader
passes easily from one chapter to the next, and even
from one section to another, without any sense of a
complete change of subject until he is well embarked
on the new voyage. This trait, which I have already
pointed out in the arrangement of the first volume,
is noticeable throughout the book. Thus, the ostrich,

The BISON

Animated Nature 3. 17, an excellent example of the sentimentalizing of **animals in** the plates of Goldsmith's book.

being most like a quadruped, serves to lighten the transition from quadrupeds to birds ; and whales, possessing, so to speak, a dual nature, introduce us less abruptly to the ' finny tribe.' From chapter to chapter this artistic coherence is everywhere apparent, and becomes what seems to me one of the most noteworthy qualities of *Animated Nature.* Moreover, Goldsmith has succeeded so well in imprinting his own individuality upon the book, that, in spite of the strange *mélange* of material he used, we are always conscious of a uniformity of tone that tells of a single, ever-present author.

This curious uniformity arises from a number of causes, the first of which is Goldsmith's continual sounding of the personal note. Like all the rest of his prose writing, *Animated Nature* abounds in pronouns of the first person singular. I have mentioned Goldsmith's practice of illustrating a fact from his personal experience, and have given a few examples from a very large number. Another trait is his introduction, often in the most unexpected places, of droll bits of humor or faint satire. Everyone knows the story of Professor Maclaurin's yawns which nearly caused a suit for libel to be brought against Nourse ; [1] but this is only one of many. For

[1] 2. 91. Goldsmith spells the professor's name ' M'Laurin.' The commonly accepted story of the incident is that given by Dr. Hill in his note to Boswell's *Life* 3. 17, where Boswell's note says that Nourse ' agreed very handsomely to have the leaf on which it was contained cancelled, and reprinted without it, at his own expence ; ' and Hill goes on to remark that ' in the second edition, published five years after Goldsmith's death, the story remains. In a footnote the editor says, that " he has been credibly informed that the professor had not the defect here mentioned." ' The fact really is, however, that the page was never cancelled, but the note was simply set at the bottom ; for my copy of the first edition is identical here with the second. If Hill looked at this page in the 1774 edition, he must have been using one of the copies struck off before the complaint was made.

instance, we meet suddenly, in the midst of an account, translated from Buffon, of the dangers that beset the wolf, this little anecdote:

> Gesner tells us of a friar, a woman, and a wolf, being taken in one of [the pitfalls], all in the same night. The woman lost her senses with fright, the friar his reputation, and the wolf his life.[1]

And then Buffon's account is resumed with: 'All these disasters, however, do not prevent this animal's multiplying in great numbers.' Again, after mentioning the excellent quality of the manati's flesh, he remarks:

> The turtle is a delicacy well known among us: our luxuries are not yet sufficiently heightened to introduce the manati; which, if it could be brought over, might singly suffice for a whole corporation.[2]

Chapter IV of Volume One is full of deft thrusts at the particular theorists whom Buffon had set Goldsmith the example of refuting. Whiston comes in for the most ridicule. Goldsmith gives us an abstract of his theory, in which it appears that, before the Flood, the internal heat of the globe had a striking effect upon the earth and its creatures:

> As its heat was then in its full power, the genial principle was also much greater than at present; vegetation and animal encrease were carried on with more vigor; and all nature seemed teeming with the seeds of life. But these physical advantages were only productive of moral evil; the warmth which invigorated the body encreased the passions and appetites of the mind; and, as man became more powerful, he grew less innocent. It was found necessary to punish his depravity; and all living creatures, except the fishes, who living

---

[1] 3. 319.
[2] 4. 186. This slightly envious attitude of Goldsmith toward luxury, so evident in many of his prose writings, and particularly in *The Deserted Village*, is several times expressed in *Animated Nature*. I shall treat it more at length in my next chapter.

in a cold element were not subject to a similitude of guilt, were overwhelmed by the deluge in universal destruction.

This deluge, which simple believers are willing to ascribe to a miracle, philosophers have long been desirous to account for by natural causes. [Here follows the account of Whiston's explanation, all in a ridiculously serious tone.] In this universal wreck of Nature Noah survived, by a variety of happy causes, to re-people the earth, and to give birth to a race of men slow in believing ill-imagined theories of the earth.[1]

The satire is never unkind, however :

> Gesner has minutely described the variety of traps by which [mice] are taken. Our Society for the Encouragement of Arts and Manufactures proposed a reward for the most ingenious contrivance for that purpose ; and I observed almost every candidate passing off [Gesner's ?] descriptions as inventions of his own. I thought it was cruel to detect the plagiarism, or frustrate the humble ambition of those who would be thought the inventors of a mouse-trap.[2]

All the little touches of humor lend life and color to the dry rehearsal of facts ; and if we add to them the continual insertion of interesting anecdotes from the accounts of travelers or from ' mere literature,' and Goldsmith's frequent ' philosophic ' disquisitions, we begin to see why *Animated Nature* makes such entertaining and coherent reading.

One other fact will complete my explanation of the unity of impression produced by *Animated Nature*. Everything Goldsmith borrows he transforms so completely that it is often well-nigh impossible, even after a careful study of his style, to know whether he is writing unhampered by a model, or is closely following an original. I spoke in the last chapter of his three methods of appropriating textual material—by direct, indirect, and a sort of abbreviated quotation which is

[1] I. 31 ff.
[2] 4. 74.

often unacknowledged—and now I shall give examples. It must be remembered at the start, however, that Goldsmith seems to have no intent to deceive his reader or misrepresent his source in thus abbreviating the matter. A chapter which he says is translated from Buffon is often shorter than the original; but anything that Goldsmith himself adds to the contents he endeavors to enclose in inverted commas, though occasionally the printer, or now and then Goldsmith himself, manages to cause a little confusion. When he does not mark a chapter as translation, it may in many places be taken very literally from the source, or may be much abbreviated, and interspersed with material from many other sources. The references in the text may be Goldsmith's own, or they may have come to him directly from the pages of Buffon, or whatever book he happens to be using. This leads one to think—and the impression is strengthened the more one studies the book—that Goldsmith usually worked without notes, sitting surrounded by books, taking what he wanted from one or another,[1] foot-notes and all, as he happened to please, now translating in his own free way, now paraphrasing, with only an occasional phrase or sentence of the original, now perhaps scrawling down a happy phrase as he happened to think of it or as it occurred in some book,[2] but always keeping clearly in mind the popular nature of his work, and the relation of the part upon which he was at the moment engaged to the whole chapter, or section, or book. One very amusing instance of his consciousness that the book is meant for a popular audience is his not infrequent habit of veiling

[1] Cf. my quotation from Cradock in the first chapter : ' . . . many books lay open that he occasionally consulted for his own materials.'

[2] Cf. the descriptions of animals scrawled on the walls, of which Boswell, and Selby's son, through Prior, have left us the record.

indelicate details from untechnical readers in perfectly lucid Latin foot-notes. We learn, for example, about the elephant :

> Multis persuasum est Elephantem non brutorum sed hominum more coire. Quod retro mingit non dubitatur. Sed ipse vidi marem hujusce speciei, in nostri regis stabulis super fæmellam itidem inclusam quadrupedum more silientem, pene paululum incurvato sed sufficienter recto.[1]

These bursts of modesty are only occasional, however ; the English text contains details which lady-like readers must have thought just as indelicate as the ones concealed from their unlearned eyes.

But let me come at once to examples of Goldsmith's borrowing. The first one illustrates how he modifies what purports to be a direct quotation from an English book :

Willughby's *Ornithology*, p. 98.	*Animated Nature* 5. 267.
I find alleged the testimony of a credible person and eye-witness, one *Theophilus Moliter*, a friend of *Fabers*, for this lurking of *Cuckows* in hollow trees. *Moliter* affirmed this to have happened at his Fathers house. His Grandfather's Servants having stocked up in a certain meadow some old, dry, rotten Willows, and brought them home, and cast the heads of two of them into the Furnace to heat the Stove, heard as it were in the Stove a *Cuckow* singing three times. Wondering at this cry of the *Cuckow* in the Winter-time, out they go,	To support the opinion that they remain torpid during the winter, at home, Willoughby introduces the following story, which he delivers upon the credit of another. ' The servants of a gentleman, in the country, having stocked up, in one of their meadows, some old dry rotten willows, thought proper, on a certain occasion, to carry them home. In heating a stove, two logs of this timber were put into the furnace beneath, and fire applied as usual. But soon, to the great surprise of the family, was heard the voice of a cuckoo, singing three times from under the stove. Wonder-

---

[1] 4. 270. This passage is particularly interesting as giving several complete sentences in Goldsmith's Latin, and also as showing his habit of observing whatever phenomena came within his notice.

and drawing the heads of the Willows out of the Furnace, in one of them they observed something move ; wherefore taking an axe they opened the hole, and thrusting in their hands, first they pluckt out nothing but meer feathers : Afterward they got hold of a living Animal, that was the very *Cuckow*, and drew it out. It was indeed brisk and lively, but wholly naked and bare of feathers, and without any Winter-provision of food, which *Cuckow* the boys kept two whole years in the Stove.

ing at so extraordinary a cry in winter-time, the servants ran and drew the willow logs from the furnace, and in the midst one of them saw something move : wherefore, taking an ax, they opened the hole, and thrusting in their hands, first they plucked out nothing but feathers ; afterwards they got hold of a living animal ; and this was the cuckoo that had waked so very opportunely for its own safety. It was, indeed,' continues our historian, ' brisk and lively, but wholly naked and bare of feathers, and without any winter provision in its hole. This cuckoo the boys kept two [misprinted *too*] years

afterwards alive in the stove; but whether it repaid them with a second song, the author of the tale has not thought fit to inform us.'

Goldsmith certainly had this passage of Willughby's before him, as the use of particular phrases like ' some old dry willows ' proves without a doubt, but he has modernized the language very neatly, without, however, quite destroying the flavor of quotation. His inclusion of a remark of his own within the quotation-marks is characteristic.

A passage from Swammerdam will serve to illustrate Goldsmith's handling of Latin :

Swammerdam, *Historia Insectorum Generalis*, pages 1-5.

Consideranti mihi, ac sæpenumero minimorum animalium naturam atque formam, maximorum naturæ ac formæ accurata judicii trutina conferenti, eæ venerunt in mentem rationes, quæ me minima ista pari dignitate non componere

Animated Nature 7. 233-234.

Those who have professedly written on this subject seem to consider it as one of the greatest that can occupy the human mind, as the most pleasing in Animated Nature. ' After an attentive examination,' says solum, verum & maximis tantum non ante ponere jusserunt. . . . Ac quemadmodum elegantissimus ille membrorum ordo, musculorum inimitabilis dispositio, venarum, arteriarum, nervorumque mirifici ductus & propagines nos jure merito in stuporem conjiciunt, quum maxima animalia curioso cultro dissecamus ; multo magis obstupescimus, ubi eadem in minimis illis ac pæne visum fugientibus animalculis adesse deprehendimus. . . . [Here Goldsmith omits a page and a half.] Imo vero licet censeantur inter minima animalcula formicæ, quid obstat, quin vel animalium majora antecellent, & in multis longo post se intervallo relinquant ; sive enim spectes sedulam earum diligentiam, sive insignem fortitudinem, sive mirificam in labore contentionem, sive stupendam illam & vix intellectu facilem στοργὴν, amorem, inquam, incredibilem, quo suos fœtus prosequuntur ; quos singulis diebus non solum in pascua, ubi alimenta idonea inveniant ; sed insuper etiam, si quo casu dissecti & in partes lacerti sint, ambabus quasi binis tenerrimo amore piissimæ hæ matres suos hosce fœtus fovendos excipiunt ; si hæc omnia spectes in tenerrimo hoc animalculo, audebisne, curiose naturæ indagator, similia ex censu majorum animalium proferre, quæ nihilominus popularis error *perfectorum* nomine donavit ? poterisne vel exemplum saltem producere, quicum ea quæ modo dixi, collata superentur ?

Swammerdam, ' of the nature and anatomy of the smallest as well as the largest animals, I cannot help allowing the least an equal, or perhaps a superior, degree of dignity. If, while we dissect with care the larger animals, we are filled with wonder at the elegant disposition of their parts, to what an height is our astonishment raised, when we discover all these parts arranged in the least in the same regular manner ! Notwithstanding the smallness of ants, nothing hinders our preferring them to the largest animals. If we consider either their unwearied diligence, their wonderful strength, or their inimitable propensity to labour. Their amazing love to their young is still more unparalleled among the larger classes. They not only daily carry them to such places as may afford them food ; but if by accident they are killed, and even cut into pieces, they, with the utmost tenderness, will carry them away piecemeal in their arms. Who can shew such an example among the larger animals, which are dignified with the title of perfect ? Who can find an instance in any other creature that can come in competition with this ? '

Here we find a stiffness, probably intentional, which, while it is not awkward enough to hinder the flow of the reading, serves to give a slightly archaic flavor quite suitable to the quotation. Goldsmith's ruthless abbreviation and freedom of translation are here particularly apparent. Notice, however, that Swammerdam's attitude is in no way misrepresented.

A bit of acknowledged translation from Buffon will complete the picture of Goldsmith as a translator :

Histoire Naturelle 2. 581

La mort n'est donc pas une chose aussi terrible que nous l'imaginons, nous la jugeons mal de loin, c'est un spectre qui nous épouvante à une certaine distance, & qui disparoit lorsqu'on vient à en approcher de près ; nous n'en avons donc que des notions fausses, nous la regardons non seulement comme le plus grand malheur, mais encore comme un mal accompagné de la plus vive douleur & des plus pénibles angoisses ; nous avons même cherché à grossir dans notre imagination ces funestes images, & à augmenter nos craintes en raisonnant sur la nature de la douleur. Elle doit être extrême, a-t-on dit, lorsque l'ame se sépare du corps, elle peut aussi être de très longue durée, puisque le temps n'ayant d'autre mesure que la succession de nos idées, un instant de douleur très-vive pendant lequel ces idées se succèdent avec une rapidité proportionnée à la violence du mal, peut nous paroître plus long qu'un siècle pendant lequel elles coulent lente-

Animated Nature 2. 206-207.

Death, therefore, is not that terrible thing which we suppose it to be. It is a spectre which frights us at a distance, but which disappears when we come to approach it more closely. Our ideas of its terrors are conceived in prejudice, and dressed up by fancy ; we regard it not only as the greatest misfortune, but as also an evil accompanied with the most excruciating tortures : we have even increased our apprehensions, by reasoning on the extent of our sufferings. It must be dreadful, say some, since it is sufficient to separate the soul from the body ; it must be long since our sufferings are proportioned to the succession of our ideas ; and these being painful, must succeed each other with entreme rapidity. In this manner has false philosophy laboured to augment the miseries of our nature ; and to aggravate that period, which Nature has kindly covered with insensibility. Neither the mind, nor

Detail from Willughby's *Ornithology*, plate 27, which contains also a peacock, a turkey, and an African hen.

ment & relativement aux senti-
mens tranquilles qui nous affec-
tent ordinairement. Quel abus
de la philosophie dans ce raisonne-
ment! Il ne mériteroit pas d'ê-
tre relevé s'il étoit sans consé-
quence, mais il influe sur le
the body, can suffer these calamities; the mind is, at that
time, mostly without ideas; and
the body too much enfeebled,
to be capable of perceiving its
pain.

malheur du genre humain, il rend l'aspect de la mort mille fois plus
affreux qu'il ne peut être, & n'y eut-il qu'on très-petit nombre
de gens trompés par l'apparence spécieuse de ces idées, il seroit
toujours utile de les détruire & d'en faire voir la fausseté.

Goldsmith's translation, then, it will be perceived,
is very free, but does not exhibit the freedom which
comes from faulty understanding of the original. I have
found that he consistently catches the exact shade of
meaning in his author, and then translates it in such
a way as not to lose the original flavor, and yet to add
to it the tone of his own style.

By Goldsmith's use of indirect quotation I mean his
practice of quoting a writer at second hand, through
the medium of some other book. One passage from
Buffon will be sufficient to illustrate this. Goldsmith
having said eight pages previously in a note: ' I have
taken four of these varieties from Linnæus; those of
the Laplanders and Tartars from Mr. Buffon,' and having
used several details from the French passage below,
proceeds, to use the quotation from Chardin, which,
since this is his only reference to that writer, has for
Goldsmith no other source than this place in Buffon:

Histoire Naturelle 3. 387.	*Animated Nat.* 2. 221-222.
Les voyageurs Hollandois s'accordent tous à dire que les Chinois ont en général le visage large, les yeux petits, le nez camus & presque point de barbe, que ceux qui sont nés à Canton & tout le long de la côte méridionale, sont aussi rasanés que les habitans de Fez en	To this race of men also, we must refer the Chinese and the Japanese, however different they seem in their manners and ceremonies . . . . There is, between these

Afrique, mais que ceux des provinces intérieures sont blancs pour la plûpart. Si nous comparons maintenant les descriptions de tous les voyageurs que nous venons de citer, avec celles que nous avons faites des Tartares, nous ne pourrons guère douter que quoiqu'il y ait de la variété dans la forme du visage & la taille des Chinois, ils n'aient cependant beaucoup plus de rapport avec les Tartares qu'avec aucun autre peuple, & que ces differences & cette variété ne viennent que du climat & du mélange des races, c'est le sentiment de Chardin : ' Les petits Tartares, dit ce voyageur, ont communément la taille plus petite de quatre pouces que la nôtre, & plus grosse à proportion ; leur teint est rouge & basané ; leurs visages sont plats, larges & carrés ; ils ont le nez écrasé & les yeux petits. Or comme ce sont là tout-à-fait les traits des habitans de la Chine, j'ai trouvé, après avoir bien observé la chose durant mes voyages, qu'il y a la même configuration de visage & de taille dans tous les peuples qui sont à l'orient & au septentrion de la mer Caspienne & à l'orient de la presqu'isle de Malaca, ce qui depuis m'a fait croire que ces divers peuples sortent tous d'une même souche, quoiqu'il paroisse des differences dans leur teint & dans leurs moeurs, car pour ce qui est du teint, la difference vient de la qualité du climat & de celle des alimens, & à l'égard des moeurs la difference vient aussi de la nature du terroir & de l'opulence plus ou moins grande.' [1]

countries, a surprising resemblance. It is in general allowed that the Chinese have broad faces, small eyes, flat noses, and scarce any beard ; that they are broad and square shouldered, and rather less in stature than Europeans. These are marks common to them and the Tartars, and they may, therefore, be considered as being derived from the same original. ' I have observed,' says Chardin, 'that in all the people from the east and the north of the Caspian sea, to the peninsula of Malacca, that the lines of the face, and the formation of the visage, is the same. This has induced me to believe, that all these nations are derived from the same original, however different either their complexions or their manners may appear : for as to the complexion, that proceeds entirely from the climate and the food ; and as to the manners, these are generally the result of their different degrees of wealth or power.'

It would have been quite characteristic for Goldsmith to have appropriated Buffon's foot-note as well as his

[1] *Amsterdam, 1711, p. 96, tome III.*   BUFFON.

quotation. This passage is an example of the inferior parts of *Animated Nature*, where the patchwork method is very apparent.

Goldsmith's third type of textual borrowing—that of abbreviated or selected, and often unacknowledged, quotation—is very frequent. Since such passages must be read entire to understand exactly how Goldsmith manages this, I shall have to content myself here with only two quotations—both taken from the history of birds, not because this kind of borrowing is any more prevalent there, but because by their comparative brevity they will be less tedious to peruse. The first is the chapter on the Dodo, which is taken principally from Buffon, though Buffon's name does not occur in it.

Histoire Naturelle, Oiseaux i. 480-484. LE DRONTE	*Animated Nature* 5. 74-76. The DODO
On regarde communément la légèreté comme un attribut propre aux oiseaux, mais si l'on vouloit en faire le caractère essentiel de cette classe, le Dronte n'auroit aucun titre pour y être admis, car loin d'annoncer la légèreté par ses proportions ou par ses mouvemens, il paroit fait exprès pour nous donner l'idée du plus lourd des êtres organisées ; représentez-vous un corps massif & presque cubique, à peine soutenu sur deux piliers très-gros & très-courts, surmonté d'une tête si extraordinaire qu'on la prendroit pour la fantaisie d'un Peintre de grotesques ; cette tête portée sur un cou renforcé & goistreux, consiste presque toute entière dans un bec énorme où sont deux gros yeux noirs entourés d'un cercle blanc, & dont l'ouverture des mandibules se prolonge bien au-delà des yeux, & presque jusqu'aux oreilles : ces deux mandibules	Mankind have generally made swiftness the attribute of birds; but the Dodo has no title to this distinction. Instead of exciting the idea of swiftness by its appearance, it seems to strike the imagination as a thing the most unwieldy and inactive of all Nature. Its body is massive, almost round, and covered with grey feathers; it is just barely supported upon two short thick legs like pillars, while its head and neck rise from it in a manner truly grotesque. The neck, thick and pursy, is joined to the head,

concaves dans le milieu de leur longeur, renflées par deux bouts & recourbées à la point en sens contraire, ressemblent à deux cuillers pointues, qui s'appliquent l'une à l'autre la convexité en dehors : de tout cela il résulte une physiognomie stupide & vorace, & qui, pour comble de difformité, est accompagnée d'un bord de plumes, lequel suivant le contour de la base du bec s'avance en pointe sur le front, puis s'arrondit autour de la face en manière de capuchon d'où lui est venu le nom de *cygne encapuchonné* (*cygnus cucullatus*).

La grosseur qui, dans les animaux, suppose la force, ne produit ici que la pesanteur ; l'autruche, le touyou, le casoar, ne sont pas plus en état de voler que le dronte, mais du moins ils sont très-vites à la course ; au lieu que le dronte paroît accablé de son propre poids, & avoir à peine la force de se traîner : c'est dans les oiseaux ce que le paresseux est dans les quadrupèdes ; on diroit qu'il est composé d'une matière brute, inactive, où les molécules vivantes ont été trop épargnées ; il a des ailes, mais ces ailes sont trop courtes & trop foibles pour l'enlever dans les airs ; il a une queue, mais cette queue est disproportionnée & hors de sa place ; on le prendroit pour une tortue qui se seroit affublée de la dépouille d'un oiseau, & la Nature en lui accordant ces ornemens inutiles, semble avoir voulu jouter l'embarras à la pesanteur, la gaucherie des mouvemens à l'inertie de la masse, & rendre sa lourde épaisseur encore plus choquante, en faisant souvenir qu'il est un oiseau.

Les premiers Hollandois qui le virent dans l'île Maurice, aujourd'hui l'île de which consists of two great chaps, that open far behind the eyes, which are large, black and prominent; so that the animal, when it gapes seems to be all mouth. The bill therefore is of an extraordinary length, not flat and broad, but thick, and of a bluish white, sharp at the end, and each chap crooked in opposite directions. They resemble two pointed spoons that are laid together by the backs. From all this results a stupid and voracious physiognomy; which is still more encreased by a bordering of feathers round the root of the beak, and which give the appearance of an hood or cowl, and finish this picture of stupid deformity. Bulk, which in other animals implies strength, in this only contributes to inactivity. The ostrich, or the cassowary, are no more able to fly than the animal before us ; but then they supply that defect by their speed in running. The dodo seems weighed down by its own heaviness, and has scarce strength enough to urge itself forward. It seems

France,[1] l'appelèrent *walg-vogel*, oiseau de dégout, autant à la cause de sa figure rebutante que du mauvais goût de sa chair ; cet oiseau bizarre est très-gros, & n'est surpassé à cet égard, que par les trois précédens car il surpasse le cygne & le dindon.

M. Brisson donne pour un de ses caractères, d'avoir la partie inférieure des jambes dénuée de plumes ; cependant la *planche CCXIX d' Edwards* le représente avec les plumes, non-seulement jusqu'au bas de la jambe, mais encore jusqu'audessous de son articulation avec le tarse ; le bec supérieur est noirâtre dans toute son étendue, excepté sur la courbure de son crochet où il y a une tache rouge ; les ouvertures des narines sont à peu près dans sa partie moyenne, tout proches de deux replis transversaux qui s'élèvent en cet endroit sur la surface.

Les plumes du front sont en général fort douces, le gris est leur couleur dominante, mais plus foncé sur toute la partie supérieure & au bas des jambes, & plus clair sur l'estomac, le ventre & tout le dessous du corps ; il y a du jaune & du blanc dans les plumes des ailes et dans celles de la queue, qui paroissent frisées, & sont en fort petit nombre. Clusius n'en compte que quatre ou cinq.

Les pieds & les doigts sont jaunes, & les ongles noirs ; chaque pied a quatre doigts, dont trois dirigés en avant & le among birds what the sloth is among quadrupedes, an unresisting thing, equally incapable of flight or defence. It is furnished with wings, covered with soft ash-coloured feathers, but they are too short to assist it in flying. It is furnished with a tail, with a few small curled feathers ; but this tail is disproportioned and displaced. Its legs are too short for running, and its body too fat to be strong. One would take it for a tortoise that had supplied itself with the feathers of a bird ; and that thus dressed out with the instruments of flight, it was only still the more unwieldy.

This bird is a native of the Isle of France ; and the Dutch, who first discovered it there, called it in their language the *nauseous bird*, as well from its disgusting figure as from the bad taste of its flesh. However, succeeding observers contradict this

---

[1] *Nota.* Les Portugais avoient auparavant nommé cette île, *Ilha do Cisne*, c'est-à-dire, *Isle aux Cygnes*, apparemment parce qu'ils y avoient aperçu des drontes qu'ils prirent pour des cygnes. *Clusius*, Exotic. *pag. 101.* BUFFON.

quatrième en arrière ; c'est celui-ci qui a l'ongle le plus long.[1]

Quelques-uns ont prétendu que le dronte avoit ordinairement dans l'estomac une pierre aussi grosse que le poing,[2] et à laquelle on n'a pas manqué d'attribuer la même origine & les mêmes vertus qu'aux bézoards ; mais Clusius qui a vu deux de ces pierres de forme et de grandeur différentes,[3] pense que l'oiseau les avoit avalées comme font les granivores, & qu'elles ne s'étoient point formées dans son estomac.

Le dronte paroît propre & particulier aux îles de France & de Bourbon, & probablement aux terres de ce continent qui en sont les moins éloignées ; mais je ne sache pas qu'aucun Voyageur ait dit l'avoir vu ailleurs que dans ces deux îles.

Quelques Hollandois l'ont nommé *dodarse* ou *dodaers* ; les Portugais & les Anglois, *dodo* ; dronte est son nom original, je veux dire celui sous lequel il est connu dans le lieu de son origine ; & c'est par cette raison que j'ai cru devoir le lui conserver, & parce qu'ordinairement des noms imposés par les peuples simples ont rapport aux propriétés de la chose nommée : on lui a encore appliqué les dénominations de *cygne à capuchon*,[4] *d'autruche encapu-*

first report, and assert, that its flesh is good and wholesome eating. It is a silly simple bird, as may very well be supposed from its figure, and is very easily taken. Three or four dodos are enough to dine an hundred men.

Whether the dodo be the same bird with that which some travellers have described under the bird of Nazareth, yet remains uncertain. The country from whence they both come is the same ; their incapacity of flying is the same ; the form of the wings and body in both are similar ; but the chief difference given is in the colour of the feathers, which in the female of the bird of Nazareth are said to be extremely beautiful ; and in the length of their legs, which in the dodo are short ; in the other, are de-

---

[1] Voyez Clusius, *Exotic. pag.* 100.—Edwards, *figure CCXIV.* BUFFON. I suspect this plate of Edwards to be the original of Goldsmith's picture of the dodo ; but there are only about 200 plates in Edwards' book, and I have not yet come upon the extra series to which Buffon must refer here.

[2] Voyage des Hollandois aux Indes Orientales, *tome III, page 214.* BUFFON.

[3] Clusius *ubi suprà.* BUFFON.

[4] Nieremberg, *Hist. nat. maxime peregrinæ*, pag. 232. BUFFON.

The DODO

Animated Nature 5. 76. Note the striking likeness to John Tenniel's Dodo, in his illustrations for *Alice in Wonderland*.

chonnée,[1] de *coq étranger*,[2] de *Walg-vogel*; & M. Moehring, qui n'a trouvé aucun de ces noms a son goût, a imaginé celui de *ruphus*, que M. Brisson a adopté pour son nom latin, comme s'il y avoit quelque avantage à donner au même animal un nom différent dans chaque langue, & comme si l'effet de cette multitude de synonymes n'étoit pas d'embarrasser la science & de jeter la confusion dans les choses : ne multiplions pas les êtres, disoient autrefois les Philosophes; mais aujourd'hui on doit dire & répéter sans cesse aux Naturalistes, ne multipliez pas les noms sans nécessité.

scribed as long. Time and future observation must clear up these doubts; and the testimony of a single witness, who shall have seen both, will throw more light on the subject than the reasonings of an hundred philosophers.

Two things I want to point out in this very interesting comparison : that Goldsmith nowhere else in this chapter —nor, if fact, anywhere near this chapter—makes the least reference to Buffon, though he translates the French account very literally at times, and that, when he has taken all he cares to take from his main source, he then makes use of whatever miscellaneous scraps of information he has acquired elsewhere.

My second example of unacknowledged quotation is in Goldsmith's chapter on rapacious birds, which is in a great measure taken from Willughby. Since the borrowing is very scattered—extending, indeed, into the next chapter as well, I shall give here only one short section :

Willughby, *Ornithology*, Book 1, Chapter 1.

Animated Nature 5. 83-84.

The Characteristic notes of Rapacious Birds in general are these : *To have a great head; a short neck; hooked, strong and sharp-pointed Beak and Talons,*

Another effect of this natural and acquired severity is, that almost all birds of prey are unsociable. It has long been observed, by Aristotle, that all

[1] Linnæus, *Gen.* 86, *spec. 4.* BUFFON.
[2] Clusius, *Exotic.* pag. 100. BUFFON.

. . . *To be very sharp-sighted,* for spying out their prey at a distance, *to be solitary, not gregarious,* by a singular providence of nature: For should they, coming in flocks, joyntly set upon Cattel, the flocks and herds of sheep and beasts would scarce be secure from their violence and injuries. This note is not common to all Rapacious birds in general, though Aristotle hath delivered for an universal observation, Γαμψωνύχων οὐδὲν ἀγελαῖον, i. e. *No Birds of prey are gregarious.* For *Vultures,* (as *Bellonius* hath observed) fly in company fifty or sixty together. . . . *The Females are of greater size, more beautiful and lovely for shape and colours, stronger, more fierce and generous than the Males.* For this cause some will have the Males called *Tarcels,* that is, *Thirds,* because they are lesser by one third part than the Females. The reason of this inequality and excess of magnitude in the Females some do assign, because it lies upon the Females to prey not only for themselves, but for their Young, therefore it is requisite that they be more strong and generous.

birds, with crooked beaks and talons, are solitary: like quadrupedes of the cat kind, they lead a lonely wandering life, and are united only in pairs, by that instinct which overpowers their rapacious habits of enmity with all other animals. As the male and female are often necessary to each other in their pursuits, so they sometimes live together; but, except at certain seasons, they most usually prowl alone; and, like robbers, enjoy in solitude the fruits of their plunder.

All birds of prey are remarkable for one singularity, for which it is not easy to account. All the males of these birds are about a third less, and weaker than the females; contrary to what obtains among quadrupedes, among which the males are always the largest and boldest: from thence the male is called, by falconers, a *tarcel;* that is, a tierce or third less than the others. . . . Whatever be the cause, certain it is, that the Females, as Willoughby expresses it, are of greater size, more beautiful and lovely for shape and colours, stronger, more fierce and generous, than the males; whether it may be that it is necessary for the female to be thus superior; as it is incumbent upon her to provide, not only for herself but her young ones also.

Here we find Goldsmith acknowledging Willughby in connection with a direct quotation, but he gives us no indication that Willughby is responsible for much more in the same chapter. The quotation from Aristotle is also directly from Willughby, just as a little later there is a quotation from Belonius through the same medium. This is the sort of borrowing that really does lay Goldsmith open to the charge of plagiarism. Nevertheless, it is very cleverly done. Almost every insertion of Goldsmith's own is admitted for the purpose of smoothing the narrative, and connecting it with the other parts of the natural history, thus tending to bind the work into a literary whole.

If my selection of quotations has not been unsuccessful, the reader is by this time fully sensible of the uniformity of tone of which I spoke at the beginning—a uniformity due, of course, principally to Goldsmith's distinctive style. I should like to pass, therefore, to a somewhat more minute examination of this style, in order to determine wherein rests its peculiar quality and evident virtue. That Goldsmith's ear was excellent is so apparent that I shall not dwell upon that point. He no doubt possessed that inherent talent for music so often observed in persons who lack the delicate muscular fitness necessary to an accomplished musician. We know that he played the flute and sang; but we have no evidence that he did either remarkably well. His great interest in things musical (witness his little essay on music inserted in the chapter on hearing in *Animated Nature*, and his essay on the Irish bard, Carolan, and many other little touches in his writing) helps to explain the really remarkable, yet unobtrusive musical quality of his prose. I do not mean to intimate, however, that his style was instinctive, and produced without effort. On the contrary, though in *Animated Nature* he is obviously writing in haste and often carelessly, his carelessness is of that justifiable kind which is made possible only by long practice. As early as 1759 he wrote to his brother Henry : ' Poetry is a much easier, and more agreeable species of composition than prose ; and could a man live by writing it, it were not unpleasant employment to be a poet ; ' and though this remark comes at the end of a somewhat jocular passage, it has the ring of truth in it. One passage in George Primrose's account of his ' philosophic vagabondage,' much of which seems to be autobiographical, throws some light upon the obscurity veiling Goldsmith's early literary career :

> I was now obliged to take a middle course, and write for bread. But I was unqualified for a profession where mere industry alone was to ensure success. I could not suppress my lurking passion for applause ; but usually consumed that time in efforts after excellence, which takes up but little room, when it should have been more advantageously employed in the diffusive productions of fruitful mediocrity. My little piece would therefore come forth in the midst of periodical publications, unnoticed and unknown. The public were more importantly employed than to observe the easy simplicity of my style, or the harmony of my periods. Sheet after sheet was thrown off to oblivion. My essays were buried among the essays upon liberty, eastern tales, and cures for the bite of a mad dog ; while Philautos, Philalethes, Philelutheros, and Philanthropos, all wrote better, because they wrote faster than I.[1]

Animated Nature was certainly written hastily in many places, but the haste is that of one who has served a long apprenticeship in the art of writing.

The fundamental virtue of Goldsmith's style is its never-failing simplicity. Whether he is speaking of the habits of an animal or of some abstruse philosophical principle, his sentences are always clear—though sometimes ungrammatical—and the thought lucid. At times

---

[1] *Vicar of Wakefield*, Chap. 20 (*Works* I. 158-159). Goldsmith's novel was first published March 27, 1766.

the tone seems a bit rhetorical, but the meaning is never obscured. Nevertheless, this apparently easy simplicity in infinitely various. It is only necessary to attempt to copy a paragraph or two to realize how seldom the phrases, which sound beautifully natural when read, are the worn-out, obvious ones. Indeed, when one first approaches Goldsmith, one regrets that his writing is not more ornamental; only after finding how easy it is to read chapter after chapter without effort, and yet without the least monotony, does one discover himself in the presence of an extremely artful prose. The simplicity gives an impression not of bareness, but of a certain exhilarating freshness.

Perhaps the chief cause of this variety is Goldsmith's delicate feeling for the exact meaning of the words he uses. In common with many other writers of his time, he stills feels the classic languages as lively realities, and, as a result, perceives in the English words derived from them a fulness of meaning which most of us can realize only by an effort of erudition. He uses synonyms with telling accuracy :

> The smallest birds avoid their pursuers by the extreme *agility*, rather than the *swiftness* of their flight; for every order would soon be at an end, if the eagle, to its own *swiftness* of wing added the *versality* of the sparrow.[1]

Another trait is the rather Johnsonian one of using two adjectives or two phrases to give full perspective to an idea. This is usually combined with a characteristic love of contrast. On one page, taken quite at random, I find :

> Such is the beauty of this creature, that it seems by Nature *fitted to satisfy* the *pride* and the *pleasure* of man; and *formed*

[1] 5. 81-82. The italics are mine. 'Versality' is apparently coined by Goldsmith.

to be taken into his service.   Hitherto, however, it appears to have disdained servitude, and neither *force* nor *kindness* have been able to wean it from its native *independence* and *ferocity*.[1]

There is, of course, much to be said against this practice when not governed by the best taste; but in Goldsmith it will seldom be found used to excess, or with the grandiosity of manner that too often inflates Johnson's prose.

Clarity and precision go far in producing a vivid style, but they do not alone account for the vivacity of Goldsmith's.   There is an immediacy about it difficult to analyze, but which I have at last come to believe is due to Goldsmith's power almost to identify himself momentarily with whatever he is describing.   For the time being, the animals are endowed with human passions; or, if you like, Goldsmith descends to their plane, and makes their actions seem as rationally motivated as those of men.   Once he has put us into this mood, the incidents he relates become vitally exciting. Here, for example, is the wicked rattlesnake charming to its death a harmless bird or squirrel:

> The snake is often seen basking at the foot of a tree, where birds and squirrels make their residence.   There, coiled upon its tail, its jaws extended, and its eyes shining like fire, the rattlesnake levels its dreadful glare upon one of the little animals above.   The bird or the squirrel, which ever it may be, too plainly perceives the mischief meditating against it, and hops from branch to branch, with a timorous, plaintive sound, wishing to avoid, yet incapable of breaking through the fascination: thus it continues for some time its feeble efforts and complaints, but is still seen approaching lower and lower towards the bottom branches of the tree, until, at last, as if overcome by the potency of its fears, it jumps down from the tree directly into the throat of its frightful destroyer.[2]

[1] 2. 392.   The italics are mine.

[2] 7. 213-214.   This account is inspired by one in the *Philosophical Transactions*.

We have here a piece of really dramatic writing; and though the cynical reader may find it childish, he can but confess it charming none the less. The fault here, of course, is that drama of this sort, which borders so nearly upon the ridiculous, is in danger of becoming melodrama; and so, in effect, it not infrequently does. An African forest is no doubt a noisy place, but scarcely quite what the tone of this passage suggests:

> Few wild animals seek their prey in the day-time; they are then generally deterred by their fears of man in the in- habited countries, and by the excessive heat of the sun in those extensive forests that lie towards the south, and in which they reign the undisputed tyrants. As soon as the morning, there- fore, appears, the carnivorous animals retire to their dens; and the elephant, the horse, the deer, and all the hare kinds, those inoffensive tenants of the plain, make their appearance. But again, at night-fall, the state of hostility begins; the whole forest then echoes to a variety of different howlings. Nothing can be more terrible than an African landscape at the close of evening: the deep toned roarings of the lion; the shriller yellings of the tiger; the jackall, pursuing by the scent, and barking like a dog; the hyæna, with a note peculiarly solitary and dreadful; but to crown all, the hissing of the various kinds of serpents, who at that time begin their call, and, as I am assured, make a much louder symphony than the birds in our groves in a morning.[1]

No small part of the effect here and in countless other passages is produced by the expression of general facts in terms of the particular. Indeed, even when making the most inclusive statements, Goldsmith presents them with so many details that he transforms the most ordinary sentences into something whose spirit is very like poetry. Here is the beginning of his introduction to the history of birds:

---

[1] 2. 320-321. I do not wish to enter into an analysis of the element of sound in Goldsmith's prose; but I must notice the almost onomatopoetic use of sound here.

> We are now come to a beautiful and loquacious race of ani-
> mals, that embellish our forests, amuse our walks and exclude
> solitude from our most shady retirements. From these man
> has nothing to fear; their pleasures, their desires, and even
> their animosities, only serve to enliven the general picture
> of Nature, and give harmony to meditation.[1]

And then again, still on the subject of birds:

> The return of spring is the beginning of pleasure. Those
> vital spirits which seemed locked up during the winter, then
> begin to expand; vegetables and insects supply abundance
> of food; and the bird having more than a sufficiency for its
> own subsistence, is impelled to transfuse life as well as to
> maintain it. Those warblings which had been hushed during
> the colder seasons, now begin to animate the fields; every
> grove and bush resounds with the challenge of anger, or the call
> of allurement. This delightful concert of the grove, which
> is so much admired by man, is no way studied for his amuse-
> ment: it is usually the call of the male to the female; his
> efforts to sooth her during the times of incubation: or it is a
> challenge between two males, for the affections of some common
> favorite.[2]

How much more charming this is in Goldsmith's prose
than if couched in the classic couplet. In short, if
I were to characterize Goldsmith's style in a sentence,
I should say that it is the style of a poet, who, being too
much of an artist to write jingling, ' poetic ' prose,
nevertheless has carried over into his prose the poet's
harmony, and the poet's use of vivid detail for the
purpose of intensifying the impression he desires to
produce.

I do not mean, of course, that the style of *Animated
Nature* is uniformly excellent. In fact, it is often
exceedingly faulty. As the reader must already have
seen from my quotations, ungrammatical constructions
are not infrequent, particularly in the latter part. I

[1] 5. 1.
[2] 5. 22.

De Seve delin   Hubert Sadp.

LE ROI DES VAUTOURS

Buffon's *Histoire Naturelle*: *Oiseaux* I. 159

have a rather numerous collection, for example, of plural subjects used with singular verbs. Occasionally the descriptions are made up of a series of facts strung together only very loosely. Now and then, also, haste of writing betrays Goldsmith into manifest absurdity. Such is the description of a polypus' banquet :

> When several polypi happen to fall upon the same worm, they dispute their common prey with each other. Two of them are often seen seizing the same worm at different ends, and dragging it at opposite directions with great force. It often happens, that while one is swallowing its respective end, the other is also employed in the same manner, and thus they continue swallowing each his part, until their mouths meet together; they then rest, each for some time in this situation, till the worm breaks between them, and each goes off with his share; but it often happens, that a seemingly more dangerous combat ensues, when the mouths of both are thus joined upon one common prey together : the largest polypus then gapes and swallows his antagonist; but what is very wonderful, the animal thus swallowed seems to be rather a gainer by the misfortune. After it has lain in the conqueror's body for about an hour, it issues unhurt, and often in possession of the prey which had been the original cause of contention ; *how happy would it be for men, if they had as little to fear from each other* ! [1]

Could moralizing possibly go farther than this ? However, in extenuation of Goldsmith, it must be said that this passage occurs very near the end of *Animated Nature*, when by many signs the author, but a few months from the end of his life as well as of his book, exhibits an utter weariness of his task. It would be unfair, also, to leave a discussion of Goldsmith's style without mentioning particularly the many eloquent passages dealing with matters more or less philosophical but, since I shall need to quote a number of them in the following chapter, I omit examples of them here.

[1] 8. 186-187. The italics are mine.

This examination of the form of *Animated Nature* shows us in Goldsmith a man endowed with really remarkable literary powers. His methods of obtaining material are often dubious, perhaps, but the result surely almost justifies him. He is a master of literary form, and has succeeded in imparting to *Animated Nature* not only a beautiful arrangement of matter, but even a uniformity of literary tone which transforms it from a mere encyclopædia of more or less reliable and interesting scientific information to something very nearly worth considering solely as a piece of literature. Although the purpose of this study is principally to use *Animated Nature* as an instrument by which to examine into the character of Goldsmith, and, therefore, is not primarily concerned with the possible influence of the book upon later writing, one would, nevertheless, be interested to know whether it did have any reflection in the literature and thought of the nineteenth century. The passage I have mentioned in *The Ancient Mariner* probably owes its origin directly to Purchas ; but, had *Animated Nature* been in Coleridge's hands instead of Purchas, we should probably have had the passage just the same. *Animated Nature* stirs the imagination at every page, even when its expression or its rampant sentimentalism makes one smile. Moreover, compilations of the type of Goldsmith's book are extremely frequent in the next century, as well as text-books of geography and science. A study of the attitude toward science and nature in the introductions to such books, as well as of their subject-matter and treatment, might conceivably show that *Animated Nature* has had a much more important effect upon the popular mind of the nineteenth century than many of the works we study for their literary value could ever pretend to have had. Without even attempting a systematic search, I have found a number of traces in such popular books,[1] either of Goldsmith's direct influence, or of a spirit similar to that which determines his attitude in *Animated Nature*. Studies, therefore, such as the present one may be useful in directing a little more of the serious attention of scholars to books which, like *Animated Nature*, are usually considered outside the realm of pure literature, and yet which may often be extremely useful in the study of literary problems.

[1] I recently stumbled upon a reference to *Animated Nature* in Melville's *Typee*, a book which would have delighted Goldsmith's heart.

CHAPTER IV

GOLDSMITH'S RELATION TO HIS AGE

Up to this point I have been treating *Animated Nature* almost as if it were an isolated literary phenomenon; but now I wish to place it in its proper setting, and from it determine how Goldsmith was affected by the various intellectual tendencies of his day. *Animated Nature* was certainly popular; and in dealing with a popular work, one very important factor to be considered is the public which gave it its reputation. No one need be reminded that popularity in itself tells nothing about the real merit of the work. Let it but fall in with the trend of the times, express what the people want expressed at the moment, and intrinsic worth is of little account; whether good or bad, it will sell. Now it is a strange and almost paradoxical fact that, though the general mass of people never wholly understand the real thinkers of their time—or indeed of any other time, they are none the less moulded in their thinking and feeling by those very thinkers. Behind the public mind of any period lies the philosophy of a few keen intellects, which, having reached the people through tortuous channels and often in weakened or distorted form, and having thus stirred at least their imaginations if not their minds, is the fundamental cause of whatever finally results from popular action. This was never more true than in the intellectually turbulent eighteenth century.

Broadly speaking, the Reformation may be called the starting-point of modern philosophy and of philosophy's offspring, modern science. Along with the new apparent freedom of the individual conscience, came the disinclination to be satisfied with revelation alone, and to use the supposedly infallible methods of mathematical logic to substantiate the as yet undoubted natural facts set forth in the Scriptures. The movement to support traditional doctrines by the unassisted reason, or else to substitute truth for them by the same means, is called rationalism. Descartes is the greatest of the founders of this school. By refusing to admit anything as true that could possibly be doubted, he arrived at the existence of three 'truths,' the ideas of which seemed to him innate in man : Mind, Matter, and God. But Locke easily showed that these ' innate ideas ' were really not innate at all, though he was still far from denying their existence. Spinoza, the ' God-intoxicated,' had, however, already thrown doubt upon the reality of matter ; Locke's argument naturally led to a fusion of matter and mind; it was but a step, then, to the complete scepticism of Hume. But absolute scepticism is too negative to attract the general mind of man ; you may deny the existence of God, and none can do much more than anathematize you; deny the reality of matter, and a Dr. Johnson can demolish your argument, for all practical purposes, by kicking a stone. The compromise which brought the problem within the scope of ordinary minds was deism.

Deism, however, when openly so called, was not popular; for it was rather a dangerous doctrine to profess. Nevertheless, deistic thought lies at the very source from which much of the English literature of the period arises. Rationalism had shown that a rationalistic God and rationalistic Matter could not mingle; if, then, we suppose a God, abstractly good and all-wise, who has created the universe, we must consider him, after that act of creation, as letting the universe act merely under the laws enacted for it at its formation. From this premise, there are two possible conclusions. Since there is undoubtedly evil and misery in the world, and since, by our premise, God can not interfere to alleviate it, we may arrive at the pessimistic conclusion that our only course is to avoid by material means as much of this misery as possible. On the other hand, if we regard evil impersonally, we may find, as Mandeville rather facetiously did, that individual vices are in reality common benefits. But neither of these is the sort of deism that much affected English popular literature.

The third variety is practically a compromise between these two views, and rests upon such a philosophical basis as that developed by Leibnitz. God, being all-good, would not do less than his utmost to create the best possible world for his creatures to inhabit. Ergo, this is the best of all possible worlds. Now, logically developed, in view of the undeniable evil in the world, this doctrine is capable of just as pessimistic an interpretation as the two former; but in the hands of illogical optimists, it became something quite different. By a slight shift of emphasis, the ' best of all possible worlds ' might be taken to mean ' a very excellent world ; ' evil could be ignored, or considered but slight in comparison with the amount of good, or else as a more or less accidental occurrence quite independent of the original plan. It is this type of deism that gave rise to the literary phenomenon of sentimentalism. Man can not endure pessimism for long ; hence, when his reason can give him little or no comfort, he is seized by the impulse of the child put to bed in the dark, who covers his head with the sheet, not because he thinks a sheet any protection against the stalkers of the night, but because it will keep him from seeing them. At the expense of truth, the sentimental *mode of thought*, for it is that rather than a philosophic doctrine, saved the eighteenth century from the wave of materialistic scepticism that swept the nineteenth.

The tenets of the sentimental faith are briefly these. Man is by nature good; but, as we find him in his civilized state, he shows much that is evil. To reconcile these two facts we must consider that his degeneration has come about because of the artificial restraints and repressions of civilization. To find the natural man—and, by hypothesis, the most nearly perfect man—we must look for him among untutored savages, or, failing the opportunity for that, among simple country-folk or otherwise uncultured and uncorrupted men; for it is there that man's natural emotions have freer, less narrowly circumscribed play; there natural goodness may flow unchecked, and ' grace may abound.' Thus sentimentalism, for the doctrine of man's fall and subsequent effort to rise, substitutes a disbelief in wilful sin, and supports the idea that by abandoning effort, rather than by increasing it, man may regain a state of perfection.

Perhaps the most striking examples of this trend of literature are to be found in the drama.[1] Men ceased going to the theatre to laugh at foibles, or to shudder at misfortune heaped upon a strong-willed man by his own fault; and there arose a new type of drama, in which tragedy became a mere struggle of nearly flawless virtue against circumstances quite outside its control, and comedy a wholesale conversion of seemingly erring characters by an appeal to their better nature—all this

[1] For this phase see Bernbaum, *Drama of Sensibility*, Boston, 1915.

usually without the least injection of a stabilizing
humor: *la gaîté est un des plus rares ornaments de la
vertu.*[1] In short, sensibility—the capacity to ' feel '—
gradually seemed to be regarded as supreme among even
the masculine virtues; and its most indubitable sign
was lachrymosity. Gushing emotion infinitely surpassed
mere intellect. Fortunately, like all extremes in art,
this one had no lack of stern opposers. Satire, particularly toward the end of the period, did not spare its
shafts;[2] and Goldsmith himself wrote both *The Good-
Natured Man* and *She Stoops to Conquer* in conscious
opposition to the modish sentimental comedy. Indeed,
the latter play was produced with great misgivings, and
occasioned by its success much surprise, and, in some
quarters, even disgust.[3] But nothing could quite stem
the tide of ' sentiment.' Sentimentalism seems inevi-
tably to destroy the power of literary discrimination,
and, in the theatre, having substituted virtuous wraiths
for real characters, finally was forced to relieve the
resulting insipidity by an appeal to the ever-present
popular liking for melodrama.[4] This taste for the
melodramatic may be traced in other kinds of writing
as well, and accounts in a measure for certain unnatural
heightenings of tone in *Animated Nature.*

Another effect of the sentimental virus, mingled
with other influences, may be seen in the enthusiastic
revival of the Il Penseroso school of poetry. Beginning
with apparently Miltonic praise of the gently pensive

[1] G. Lanson, *Nivelle de la Chaussée et la Comédie Larmoyante.*

[2] R. C. Whitford, ' Satire's View of Sentimentalism in the Days
of George the Third ' (*Journal of English and Germanic Philology*
18 (1919). 155-204).

[3] E. g., Horace Walpole.

[4] Note, for example, the mere titles of plays in any thirty pages
of Garrick's *Correspondence.*

mood, urged on by the example of certain Elizabethan writers who talk of death and the cankering worm, and led further, perhaps, by the fundamental hopelessness of the insidious deism, certain poets indulged in a riot of graveyards and charnel-houses—always, at this period, with an apparent moral purpose, but likewise with an undeniable joy in their subject-matter.[1] And, when combined with the interest of the period in primitive man as an exemplification of natural virtue, this tendency produced Macpherson's *Ossian*, with its misty landscapes, wailing ghosts, meteors, and ' joy of grief.'[2] So examples of the influence of the sentimental faith might be endlessly multiplied—the faith which not merely affected those who would have acquiesced in the philosophical precepts at its basis, but tainted even those who would most strenuously have opposed its premises; for it had indeed become, as Leslie Stephen says, ' a kind of mildew which spreads over the surface of literature at this period to indicate a sickly constitution.'[3]

But sentimentalism, for all its vogue, never quite overcame neo-classicism, which was most favorably exemplified at this time, perhaps, by Samuel Johnson.[4]

---

[1] Parnell's *Night Piece on Death*, Blair's *Grave*, Young's *Night Thoughts*, etc., culminating in Gray's *Elegy*, which once for all revealed the other influence upon this melancholic mood : the growing insistence of the *bourgeoisie* upon its equality with the upper classes—an equality which it found, if nowhere else, at least in death.

[2] See Hugh Blair's *Critical Dissertation on the Poems of Ossian,* than which I know no more perfect summary of all that pleased the sentimental taste of Goldsmith's time.

[3] *History of English Thought in the 18th Century* 2. 436.

[4] Johnson's position is perhaps more truly classic than that of many others of the school. He did not, for example, share the general dislike of Goldsmith's bailiff scenes.

Goldsmith had run a tilt with the less progressive suppor-
ters of this school in the bailiff scenes of *The Good-
Natured Man*, which public opinion had stamped as
' low '; but he was, if only by virtue of his association
with Johnson, classic in many of his tendencies. This
part of the public demanded first of all in a writer that
he be learned; that is, that he be well-read in the
classics, and not scruple to show it in his book. His
language must be 'elegant', and must lift even ordinary
things into a refined atmosphere. A work written in
the sentimental vein would sell to the middle classes;
one learnedly and loftily written would attract · their
betters; but, to suit both parties, it would have to combine at least the appearance of sentimentalism with
a more or less substantiated claim to learning and
elegance of style.

There is still another side to this most interesting of
centuries. Experimental science had been making great
strides since the time of Descartes; new lands had been
discovered and great explorations made, so that men
were at last beginning to arrive at a more or less accurate knowledge of the physical universe. But, as is
shown by the use of the term ' philosophy ' to cover
almost all knowledge and research not purely literary
or linguistic, they had not yet realized the impossibility
of every man's attaining excellence in every department
of knowledge; specialization, with all its attendant
evils and benefits, was reserved for the next century.
The desire to combine the essentials of knowledge into
one book seems as old as the art of writing itself; but
the eighteenth century was particularly moved in that
direction. Thus we have compendious books of travel,
compendious histories,[1] the *Encyclopédie* in France, an

---

[1] E. g., Goldsmith's own.

attempt at an industrial encyclopædia,[1] Buffon's *Histoire Naturelle, Animated Nature* itself, and Goldsmith's projected *Survey of Experimental Science,* to mention no more. All this displays the growing activity of public curiosity, which, though none too scrupulous as to the veracity of the information which it received, nevertheless, by putting a premium on discovery, was surely doing much to further the advance of science.

With such a public as the eighteenth century provided, there is every reason why a natural history from the pen of a man like Goldsmith should be popular. Descartes had long before shown how little difference there was between the behavior of men and of animals ; and now animals were becoming more and more important as indices of the actions of man in his primitive state. A natural history, dealing as it must with outlandish regions, appealed to the reader who delighted in books of travel, giving him in compendious form the cream of many volumes. To the tyro in science, Goldsmith, with his medical knowledge, spoke with a certain amount of authority, and to those who knew more than he, he was doing the service of collecting and arranging material in convenient form. Finally, having more than once proved his right to the title of ' learned ', and, as

---

[1] The executor of this lengthy series was Henri Louis Duhamel de Monceau. Goldsmith is obviously referring to this work when he says (2. 308) : ' We have lately seen a laborious work carried on at Paris, with this only intent of teaching all the trades by description ; however, the design at first blush seems to be ill considered ; and it is probable that very few advantages will be derived from so laborious an undertaking. With regard to the descriptions in natural history, these, without all question, under the direction of good sense, are necessary ; but still they should be kept within proper bounds ; and, where a thing may be much more easily shewn than described, the exhibition should ever precede the account.'

we shall see, writing in a way not unattractive to the sentimentalists, he could scarcely help pleasing a very large audience.

One very obvious connection of Goldsmith with the sentimental school of thought is found in his *Deserted Village*. Taken by itself this poem is rather startling, for, in reading Goldsmith's other well known works, we find little to prepare us for this apparently sudden championing of the poor against the economic oppressions which result, as Goldsmith thinks, from the selfish luxury of the upper classes. *Animated Nature* shows us, however, that this idea was continually present in Goldsmith's mind :

> The hunting of the sable chiefly falls to the lot of the con-
> demned criminals, . . . and in this instance, as in many others,
> the luxuries and ornaments of the vain, are wrought out of the
> dangers and the miseries of the wretched. These are obliged
> to furnish a certain number of skins every year, and are
> punished if the proper quantity be not provided.[1]

Goldsmith classes the cow as the chief of ruminating animals because of her beauty and serviceableness, and again airs his opinions on luxury :

> There are many of our peasantry that have no other possess-
> ions but a cow ; and even of the advantages resulting from this
> most useful creature, the poor are but nominal possessors.
> Its flesh they cannot pretend to taste, since then their whole
> riches are at once destroyed ; its calf they are obliged to fatten
> for sale, since veal is a delicacy they could not make any pre-
> tensions to ; its very milk is wrought into butter and cheese
> for the tables of their masters ; while they have no share even
> in their own possession, but the choice of their market, I cannot
> bear to hear the rich crying out for liberty, while they thus
> starve their fellow-creatures, and feed them up with an im-
> aginary good, while they monopolize the real benefits of Nature.
> In those countries where the men are under better subordina-
> tion, this excellent animal is of more general advantage. In

[1] 3. 375.

The King of the Vultures

Animated Nature 5. 107

Germany, Poland, and Switzerland, every peasant keeps two or three cows, not for the benefit of his master, but for himself. The meanest of the peasants there kills one cow at least for his own table, which he salts and hangs up, and thus preserves as a delicacy all the year round. There is scarce a cottage in those countries that is not hung round with these marks of hospitality; and which often make the owner better contented with hunger, since he has it in his power to be luxurious when he thinks proper. A piece of beef hung up there, is considered as an elegant piece of furniture, which, though seldom touched, at least argues the possessor's opulence and ease. But it is very different, for some years past, in this country, where our lower rustics at least are utterly unable to purchase meat at any part of the year, and by them even butter is considered as an article of extravagance.[1]

The superiority of rural life on the continent is further emphasized in considering the sheep:

In those countries that still continue poor, the Arcadian life is preserved in all its former purity; but in countries where a greater inequality of conditions prevail, the shepherd is generally some poor wretch who attends a flock from which he is to derive no benefits, and only guards those luxuries which he is not fated to share.[2]

Owners of the goat, however, usually fare better than those of the cow:

In several parts of Ireland, and the highlands of Scotland, the goat makes the chief possession of the inhabitants. On those mountains, where no other useful animal could find subsistence, the goat continues to glean a sufficient living; and supplies the hardy natives with what they consider as varied luxury. They lie upon beds made of their skins, which are soft, clean, and wholesome; they live upon their milk, with oat bread; they convert a part of it into butter, and some into cheese; the flesh, indeed, they seldom taste of, as it is a delicacy which they find too expensive; however the kid is considered, even by the city epicure, as a great rarity; and the

[1] 3. 8-9.
[2] 3. 42.

flesh of the goat, when properly prepared, is ranked by some
as no way inferior to venison. In this manner, even in the
wildest solitudes, the poor find comforts of which the rich do
not think it worth their while to dispossess them; in these
mountainous retreats, where the landscape presents only a
scene of rocks, heaths, and shrubs, that speak the wretchedness of the soil, these simple people have their feasts, and their
pleasures; their faithful flock of goats attends them to these
awful solitudes, and furnishes them with all the necessaries of
life; while their remote situation happily keeps them ignorant
of greater luxury.[1]

Civilization, however, is not wholly harmful in its effects,
as we learn if we consider the condition of the peasantry
at the time when the nobles kept large game-preserves,
and otherwise hampered agriculture. The solution of
the problem is evidently the institution of a common-
wealth which looks after the interests of *all* its members:

When property became more equally divided, by the introduction of arts and industry, these extensive hunting grounds
became more limited; and as tillage and husbandry increased,
the beasts of chace were obliged to give way to others more
useful to community. Those vast tracts of land, before dedicated to hunting, were then contracted; and, in proportion as
the useful arts gained ground, they protected and encouraged
the labours of the industrious, and repressed the licentiousness
of the sportsman. It is, therefore, among the subjects of a
despotic government only that these laws remain in full force,
where large wastes lie uncultivated for the purposes of hunting,
where the husbandman can find no protection from the in-
vasions of his lord, or the continual depredations of these
animals which he makes the objects of his pleasure.[2]

There are, however, some few things which the poor
in any state of society may enjoy in equality with the
wealthy:

[Air] is an element of which Avarice will not deprive us;
and which Power cannot monopolize. The treasures of the

[1] 3. 55-56.
[2] 3. 111.

earth, the verdure of the fields, and even the refreshments of the stream, are too often seen going only to assist the luxuries of the great; while the less fortunate part of mankind stand humble spectators of their encroachments. But the air no limitations can bound, nor any land-marks restrain. In this benign element, all mankind can boast an equal possession; and for this we all have equal obligations to Heaven. We consume a part of it, for our own sustenance, while we live; and, when we die, our putrefying bodies give back the supply, which, during life, we had accumulated from the general mass.[1]

This sympathy of Goldsmith for the sufferings of the poor, however unsound it may be as social philosophy, is easily explained when we remember the 'scurvy circumstances' he so frequently himself had to endure. His discussion of hunger, for example, has the tone of personal experience. 'It is so terrible to man,' says he, 'that to avoid it he even encounters certain death; and, rather than endure its tortures, exchanges them for immediate destruction.'[2] Then after various accounts of cases of starvation, he continues:

However this may be, we have but few instances of men dying, except at sea, of absolute hunger. The decline of those unhappy creatures who are destitute of food, at land, being more slow and unperceived. These, from often being in need, and as often receiving an accidental supply, pass their lives between surfeiting and repining; and their constitution is impaired by insensible degrees. Man is unfit for a state of precarious expectation. That share of provident precaution which incites him to lay up stores for a distant day, becomes his torment, when totally unprovided against an immediate call. The lower race of animals, when satisfied, for the instant moment, are perfectly happy: but it is otherwise with man; his mind anticipates distress, and feels the pangs of want even before it arrests him. Thus the mind, being continually

[1] 1. 335-336. Notice how this reflects the 'Graveyard Poets', and confirms the statement that one large element of sentimentalism is the desire of the *bourgeoisie* for equality.

[2] 2. 125

harrassed by the situation, it at length influences the constitution, and unfits it for all its functions.   Some cruel disorder,
but no way like hunger, seizes the unhappy sufferer; so ·that
almost all those men who have thus long lived by chance,
and whose every day may be considered as an happy escape
from famine, are known at last to die in reality, of a disorder
caused by hunger; but which, in the common language, is
often called a *broken-heart*. Some of these I have known
myself, when very little able to relieve them; and I have been
told, by a very active and worthy magistrate, that the number
of such as die in London for want, is much greater than one
would imagine— I think he talked of two thousand in a year.[1]

All this is no doubt sentimental; but we can forgive
the tears of the sentimentalist who has himself endured
the ills for which he sheds them.

Goldsmith's evident sympathy with the sufferings of
animals connects him with another of the nobler phases
of sentimentalism.   In Goldsmith this feeling is abso-
lutely sincere, as we can not say of all the sentimentalists in an age which drew upon itself such a rebuke
as Hogarth's *Progress of Cruelty*.   There are in *Animated
Nature* many accounts of hunting, but Goldsmith is
not over fond of the sport, at least as it is practised in
civilized countries, and more often than not shows that
his sympathy is with the hunted:

In England . . . [the stag] is driven from some gentleman's
park, and then hunted through the open country. But those
who pursue the wild animal, have a much higher object, as
well as a greater variety in the chace.   To let loose a creature
that was already in our possession, in order to catch it again,
is, in my opinion, but a poor pursuit, as the reward, when
obtained, is only what we before had given away. But to
pursue an animal that owns no proprietor, and which he that
first seizes may be said to possess, has something in it that
seems at least more rational; this rewards the hunter for his
toil, and seems to repay his industry. Besides, the superior

[1] 2. 128-130.

strength and swiftness of the wild animal prolongs the amusement; it is possessed of more various arts to escape the hunter,
and leads him to precipices where the danger ennobles the chace.
In pursuing the animal let loose from a park, as it is unused
to danger, it is but little versed in the stratagems of escape;
the hunter follows as sure of overcoming, and feels none of those
alternations of hope and fear which arise from the uncertainty
of success. But it is otherwise with the mountain stag : having
spent his whole life in a state of continual apprehension ; having
frequently been followed, and as frequently escaped, he knows
every trick to mislead, to confound, or intimidate his pur-
suers ; to stimulate their ardour, and enhance their success.[1]

The slandered ' mad ' dog calls forth his defense also :

[Rabies] is a disorder by no means so frequent as the terrors
of the timorous would suppose ; the dog has been often accused
of madness, without a fair trial; and some persons have been
supposed to receive their deaths from his bite, when either
their own ill-grounded fears, or their natural disorders were
the true cause.[2]

In his description of the cat Goldsmith follows Buffon
rather closely, and thus is led, apparently before he
realizes it, into an endorsement of the French philosopher's emphatic disapproval of that animal. Accordingly, after giving Buffon's account of the cat's selfish,
cowardly, and luxurious habits, Goldsmith thus excuses
the creature :

Many of its habits, however, are rather the consequences
of its formation, than the result of any perverseness in its
disposition; it is timid and mistrustful, because its body is
weak, and its skin tender ; a blow hurts it infinitely more than
it does a dog, whose hide is thick and body muscular ; the
long fur in which the cat is clothed, entirely disguises its shape,
which, if seen naked, is long, feeble, and slender ; it is not to

---

[1] 3. 112-113.
[2] 3. 305. Goldsmith several times speaks thus of the ' mad
dog, as, for example, in Letter 68 of *The Citizen of the World*,
and in the *Elegy on the Death of a Mad Dog*.

be wondered, therefore, that it appears much more fearful
of chastisement than the dog, and often flies, even when no
correction is intended. Being also the native of the warmer
climates, as will be shown hereafter, it chooses the softest
bed to lie on, which is always the warmest.[1]

In short, Goldsmith possessed a heart so tender that
it was never proof against the appeal of weakness and
distress, whether from a poor fellow-mortal begging the
'loan of a chamber-pot full of coals,' or from a dumb
animal maligned by a cruel world.

But an excess even of true sensibility is likely to lead
now and then to something that approaches perilously
near to the specious. Goldsmith's tendency to humanize
animals I have noted in my treatment of his style,
because it had an obvious effect upon the tone of *Animated Nature*; but the discussion of this trait belongs
more properly in this place. The attribution of human
sensations and passions to the lower animals has been
common in all times; but usually the purpose was satire
or sheer fantasy. The sentimentalist, however, in his
search for the primitive, began in deadly seriousness
to regard animals not as the modern scientist does—as
creatures whose desires and abilities are suited to their
environment, but rather as creatures susceptible to
human desires, and yet only very partially capable of
satisfying them; that is, they consider them so when
they forget for the time that animals, being nearer the
primitive and the natural, are, according to the sentimental doctrine, nearer perfection. Contradiction is
rampant wherever the sentimentalist treats of animals
—not so much, however, contradiction of fact as contradiction of interpretation. Goldsmith regards some animals as gentle and ' inoffensive,' some as laborious, some

[1] 3. 203.

as cruel and tyrannous. The number of 'lords' of various departments of nature is astounding. The lion, of course, holds undisputed sway in the forests where he resides, but we learn also that the elephant is equally supreme. Nevertheless, the monkey ventures to set the power of both of these at naught, and even he, as we find immediately afterward, is not perfectly free from opposition :

> There is but one animal in all the forest that ventures to oppose the monkey, and that is the serpent. The larger snakes are often seen winding up the trees where the monkeys reside; and, when they happen to surprise them sleeping, swallow them whole before the little animals have time to make a defence. In this manner, the two most mischievous kinds in all Nature keep the whole forest between them ; both equally formidable to each other, and for ever employed in mutual hostilities. The monkeys in general inhabit the tops of the trees, and the serpents cling to the branches nearer the bottom ; and in this manner they are for ever seen near each other, like enemies in the same field of battle. Some travellers, indeed, have supposed that their vicinity rather argued their mutual friendship, and that they united in this manner to form an offensive league against all the rest of animated Nature.[1] ' I have seen these monkeys,' says Labat, ' playing their gambols upon those very branches on which the snakes were reposing, and jumping over them without receiving any injury, although the serpents of that country were naturally vindictive, and always ready to bite whatever disturbed them.' These gambols, however were probably nothing more than the insults of an enemy that was conscious of its own safety ; and the monkeys might have provoked the snake in the same manner as we often see sparrows twitter at a cat. However this be, the forest is generally divided between them ; and these woods, which Nature seems to have embellished with her richest magnificence, rather inspire terror than delight, and chiefly serve as retreats for mischief and malignity.[2]

[1] Labat, Relat. de l'Afriq. Occident, p. 317.   GOLDSMITH. 4. 219-221.

These various autocracies are, I suppose, credible; but
when the white bear, the hippopotamus, the rhinoceros,
and even the seal are in turn proclaimed monarch each
of his particular realm, one begins to wonder whether
'Nature's perfect plan' may not be perfect anarchy.

The beasts of prey are 'a bloody and unrelenting
tribe, that disdain to own [man's] power, and carry on
unceasing hostilities against him.' 'All the fiercest of
the carnivorous kinds seek their food in gloomy solitude.'

> They are, in general, fierce, rapacious, subtle, and cruel, unfit
> for society among each other, and incapable of adding to
> human happiness. However, it is probable that even the
> fiercest could be rendered domestic, if man thought the con-
> quest worth the trouble. Lions have been yoked to the chariots
> of conquerors, and tigers have been taught to tend those
> herds which they are known at present to destroy; but these
> services are not sufficient to recompence for the trouble of
> their keeping; so that ceasing to be useful, they continue to
> be noxious, and become rebellious subjects because not taken
> under equal protection with the rest of the brute creation.[1]

Some animals have dispositions of an even less agreeable kind:

> The fox or the wolf are for ever prowling; their long habits
> of want give them a degree of sharpness and cunning; their
> life is a continued scene of stratagem and escape.[2]

And even the other animals dislike them:

> so that it is the fate of this petty plunderer [the fox] to be
> detested by every rank of animals; all the weaker classes
> shun, and all the stronger pursue him.[3]

This opinion, however, does not prevent Goldsmith from
telling the following anecdote:

[1] 3. 198-199.
[2] 3. 2.
[3] 3. 332.

A remarkable instance of this animal's parental affection happened while I was writing this history in the county of Essex. A she-fox that had, as it should seem, but one cub, was unkennelled by a gentleman's hounds, near Chelmsford, and hotly pursued. In such a case, when her own life was in imminent peril, one would think it was not a time to consult the safety of her young; however, the poor animal, braving every danger, rather than leave her cub behind to be worried by the dogs, took it up in her mouth, and ran with it in this manner for some miles. At last, taking her away [way?] through a farmer's yard, she was assaulted by a mastiff, and at last obliged to drop her cub, which was taken up by the farmer. I was not displeased to hear that this faithful creature escaped the pursuit, and at last got off in safety.[1]

The gentler virtues are certainly not lacking in the animal world. The ostriches, for example,

lead an inoffensive and social life; the male, as Thevenot assures us, assorting with the female with connubial fidelity.[2]

In fact, the birds are usually less offensive than the other classes of animated nature, as we see, for instance, in the cassowary:

Thus formed for a life of hostility, for terrifying others, and for its own defence, it might be expected that the cassowary was one of the most fierce and terrible animals of the creation. But nothing is so opposite to its natural character, nothing so different from the life it is contented to lead. It never attacks others; and instead of the bill, when attacked, it rather makes use of its legs, and kicks like a horse, or runs against its pursuer, beats him down, and treads him to the ground.[3]

The stag, too, is commendable for his elegant disposition and demeanor:

[1] 3. 330.

[2] 5. 56.

[3] 5. 71. It might be queried whether simple biting would in the end be less gentle than this.

The stag is one of those innocent and peaceable animals that seems made to embellish the forest, and animates the solitudes of Nature. The easy elegance of his form, the lightness of his motions, those large branches that seem made rather for the ornament of his head than its defence, the size, the strength, and the swiftness of this beautiful creature, all sufficiently rank him among the first of quadrupedes, among the most noted objects of human curiosity.[1]

It is reserved, however, for the elephant to show himself the Sir Charles Grandison of the animal world; not only does he possess all the noble virtues, but he reveals in himself also that delicate sensibility demanded of a man of refinement :

This animal's sense of smelling is not only exquisite, but it is in a great measure pleased with the same odours that delight mankind. The elephant gathers flowers with great pleasure and attention; it picks them up one by one, unites them into a nosegay, and seems charmed with the perfume.[2]

Some animals, judged by human standards, ought to be supremely miserable, and so Goldsmith seems to conceive them, though, apparently somewhat to his surprise, Nature has given them compensation. One of these animals is the mole :

Were we from our own sensations to pronounce upon the life of a quadrupede that was never to appear above ground, but always condemned to hunt for its prey underneath, obliged, whenever it removed from one place to another, to bore its way through a resisting body, we should be apt to assert that such an existence must be the most frightful and solitary in Nature. However, in the present animal, though we find it condemned to all those seeming inconveniences, we shall discover no sign of wretchedness or distress. No quadrupede, is fatter, none has a more sleek or glossy skin ; and, though

[1] 3. 94.

[2] 4. 258-259. I do not find Goldsmith's source for this striking picture.

Sexe Del.

Chevillet Sculp.

LE JOCKO.

Buffon's *Histoire Naturelle* 14. 82. See above, page 59.

denied many advantages that most animals enjoy, it is more liberally possessed of others, which they have in a more scanty proportion.[1]

The nature of these advantages we learn a few pages further on :

> The wants of a subterraneous animal can be but few ; and these [sense-organs] are sufficient to supply them : to eat, and to produce its kind, are the whole employment of such a life; and for both these purposes it is wonderfully adapted by Nature.[2]

And then, lest we mistake his meaning, Goldsmith adds this foot-note :

> * Testes habet maximos, parastatas amplissimas, novum corpus seminale ab his diversum ac separatum. Penem etiam facile omnium, ni fallor, animalium longissimum, ex quibus colligere est maximam præ reliquis omnibus animalibus volup- tatem in coitu, hoc objectum et vile animalculum percipere, ut habeant quod ipsi invideant qui in hoc supremas vitæ suæ delicias collocant : Raii Synops. Quadru. p. 239. Huic opinioni assentitur D. Buffon, attamen non mihi apparet

---

[1] 4. 90-91.

[2] 4. 94-95. An interesting parallel to this is found in the chapter, ' Of Sleep and Hunger ' (2. 123) : ' As man, in all the privileges he enjoys, and the powers he is invested with, has a superiority over all other animals, so, in his necessities, he seems inferior to the meanest of them all.   Nature has brought him into life with a greater variety of wants and infirmities, than the rest of her crea- tures, unarmed in the midst of enemies. . . .   Every want thus becomes a means of pleasure, in the redressing ; and the animal that has more desires, may be said to be capable of the greatest variety of happiness.'   This is, in turn, an echo of *The Traveller* (209-214) :

> Such are the charms to barren states assign'd :
> Their wants but few, their wishes all confin'd :
> Yet let them only share the praises due,—
> If few their wants, their pleasures are but few ;
> For every want that stimulates the breast,
> Becomes a source of pleasure when redrest.'

magnitudinem partium talem voluptatem augere. Maribus
salacissimis contrarium obtinet.[1]

Moreover, its apparent defects may in fact be real
advantages :

> The smallness of its eyes, which induced the ancients to
> think it was blind, is, to this animal, a peculiar advantage.
> A small degree of vision is sufficient for a creature that is ever
> destined to live in darkness. A more extensive sight would
> only have served to shew the horrors of its prison, while Nature
> had denied it the means of an escape.

But the sloth is of all creatures apparently the most
miserable, and so far below the human level that it is
practically impossible to understand why it was created :

> How far these may be considered as the unfinished produc-
> tions of Nature, I will not take upon me to determine; if we
> measure their happiness by our sensations, nothing, it is certain,
> can be more miserable; but it is probable, considered with
> regard to themselves, they may have some stores of comfort
> unknown to us, which may set them upon a level with some
> other inferior ranks of the creation; if a part of their life be
> exposed to pain and labour, it is compensated by a larger
> portion of plenty, indolence, and safety. In fact, they are
> formed very differently from all other quadrupedes, and it
> is probable, they have different enjoyments.[2]

Thus it is almost impossible for Goldsmith to conceive
the scientific fact that physical happiness really consists
in fitness to environment, rather than in any particular intellectual or nervous sensations.

The most fortunate and the most commendable animals, however, are those which man has thought fit to
take under his dominion. This is the inevitable out-
come of a train of thought which starts with the premise

---

[1] As I have said, Goldsmith never scruples to disagree with his
authorities when his own observation has better informed him.
[2] 4. 346.

that the importance of anything in the universe can be measured only by the service it renders to man. In passing from the ruminating animals to those of the cat tribe, Goldsmith says :

> We have hitherto been describing a class of peaceful and harmless animals, that serve as the instruments of man's happiness, or at least that do not openly oppose him.[1]

Opposition to man's will is, then, a scarcely pardonable fault. Some animals are wiser than to resist their heaven-ordained master :

> Both [the sheep and the goat] seem to require protection from man ; and are, in some measure, pleased with his society. The sheep, indeed, is the more serviceable creature of the two ; but the goat has more sensibility and attachment. The attending upon both was once the employment of the wisest and the best of men ; and those have been ever supposed the happiest times, in which these harmless creatures were considered as the chief objects of human attention. In the earliest ages, the goat seemed rather the greater favourite ; and, indeed, it continues such to this day among the poor. However, the sheep has long since become the principal object of human care ; while the goat is disregarded by the generality of mankind, or become the possession only of the lowest of the people.[2]

This feeling that animals enjoy their servitude is repeated again and again. We hear of the ' fond submission ' of the horse, and of the remarkable faithfulness of the ass in the face of every insult, and even of the friendliness of animals which might be supposed to have some backward longing for their former freedom. The Hottentot possesses such a treasure :

> But it is among the Hottentots where these animals [bisons] are chiefly esteemed, as being more than commonly serviceable. They are their fellow-domestics, the companions of their plea-

---

[1] 3. 198.
[2] 3. 37.

sures and fatigues ; the cow is at once the Hottentot's protector
and servant, assists him in attending his flocks, and guarding
them against every invader ; while the sheep are grazing, the
faithful *backely*, as this kind of cow is called, stands or grazes
beside them : still, however, attentive to the looks of its master,
the backely flies round the field, herds in the sheep that are
straying, obliges them to keep within proper limits, and shews
no mercy to robbers, or even strangers, who attempt to plunder.
But it is not the plunderers of the flock alone, but even the
enemies of the nation, that these backelys are taught to combat.
Every army of the Hottentots is furnished with a proper herd
of these, which are let loose against the enemy, when the
occasion is most convenient. Being thus sent forward, they
overturn all before them ; they strike every opposer down
with their horns, and trample upon them with their feet ; and
thus often procure their masters an easy victory, even before
they have attempted to strike a blow. An animal so ser-
viceable, it may be supposed, is not without its reward. The
backely lives in the same cottage with its master, and, by
long habit, gains an affection for him ; and in proportion as
the man approaches to the brute, so the brute seems to attain
even to some share of human sagacity. The Hottentot and
his backely thus mutually assist each other ; and when the
latter happens to die, a new one is chosen to succeed him, by
a council of the old men of the village. The new backely is
then joined with one of the veterans of his own kind, from
whom he learns his art, becomes social and diligent, and is
taken for life into human friendship and protection.[1]

Goldsmith seems to approve the use of the backely
in war ; but he is later to say :

It were happy indeed for man, if, while converting these
quadrupedes [horses, elephants, etc.] to his own benefit, he
had not turned them to the destruction of his fellow-creatures ;
he has employed some of them for the purposes of war, and they
have conformed to his noxious ambition with but too fatal
an obedience.[2]

Such discrepancies reveal a contradiction in connection

[1] 3. 21-22.
[2] 4. 354.

with this matter of the domestication of animals which is due, as it seems to me, not primarily to Goldsmith, but rather to the general sentimental attitude toward them. Immediately following the quotation I have given concerning the sheep and the goat occurs this passage:

> Those animals that take refuge under the protection of man, in a few generations become indolent and helpless. Having lost the habit of self-defence, they seem to lose also the instincts of Nature. The sheep, in its present domestic state, is of all animals the most defenceless and inoffensive. With its liberty it seems to have been deprived of its swiftness and cunning; and what in the ass might rather be called patience, in the sheep appears to be stupidity. With no one quality to fit it for self-preservation, it makes vain efforts at all. Without swiftness, it endeavours to fly; and without strength, sometimes offers to oppose. But these feeble attempts rather incite than repress the insults of every enemy; and the dog follows the flock with greater delight upon seeing them fly, and attacks them with more fierceness upon their unsupported attempts at resistance. Indeed, they run together in flocks; rather with the hopes of losing their single danger in the crowd, than of uniting to repress the attack by numbers. The sheep, therefore, were it exposed in its present state to struggle with its natural enemies of the forest, would soon be extirpated. Loaded with an heavy fleece, deprived of the defence of its horns, and rendered heavy, slow, and feeble, it can have no other safety than what it finds from man. This animal is now, therefore, obliged to rely solely upon that art for protection, to which it originally owes its degradation.[1]

But we are not to impute to Nature,' continues Goldsmith, ' the formation of an animal so utterly unprovided against its enemies, and so unfit for defence;' and then he goes on to show how different are the various kinds of undomesticated sheep:

> It is by human art alone that the sheep is become the tardy defenceless creature we find it. Every race of quadru-

---

[1] 3. 38-39.

pedes might easily be corrupted by the same allurements by
which the sheep has been thus debilitated and depressed.

As Goldsmith shows again and again, the influence of
man always has a deleterious effect upon wild animals.
' In all countries, as man is civilized and improved, the
lower ranks of animals are repressed and degraded.' [1]
Even the beaver becomes less clever and industrious
when interfered with by man. Goldsmith, moreover,
in these statements reveals a real sympathy for the
brutes thus degraded for the benefit of mankind, and
even wonders occasionally whether man has the right
thus to destroy the happiness of other living creatures
in order to increase his own. However, the general
opinion of his day is too strong for him, and convinces
him that man is the centre of the universe, and all
things become important only as they pertain to him.
We find him, therefore, ending his remarks on the
sheep thus :

> Such is the sheep in its savage state ; a bold, noble, and even
> beautiful animal : but it is not the most beautiful creatures
> that are always found most useful to man. Human industry
> has therefore destroyed its grace, to improve its utility.

Every sort of animal can be shown to be advantageous
to man :

> Were it not for the lion, the tiger, the panther, the rhi-
> noceros, and the bear, he would scarce know his own powers,
> and the superiority of human art over brutal fierceness. These
> serve to excite, and put his nobler passions into motion. [2]

And as these

> call forth [misprinted ' are called forth'] his boldest efforts,
> so the numerous tribe of the smaller vermin kind excite his
> continual vigilance and caution.

[1] 4. 157.
[2] 4. 355.

The OURAN OUTANG

Animated Nature 4. 189.   See above, page 59.

Finally, our only reason for studying quadrupeds is that they are invaluable to man:

> All knowledge is pleasant only as the object of it contributes to render man happy, and the services of quadrupedes being so very necessary to him in every situation, he is particularly interested in their history: without their aid, what a wretched and forlorn creature would he have been! the principal part of his food, his clothing, and his amusements are derived wholly from them; and he may be considered as a great lord, sometimes cherishing his humble dependents, and sometimes terrifying the refractory, to contribute to his delight and conveniences.[1]

This last phase shows less of the influence of sentimentalism, and more of that of the still thriving neoclassicism. Indeed, we should scarcely expect anything else from a friend of Samuel Johnson. 'The proper study of mankind is man;' and so the only means natural history has of justifying itself is to show how everything it deals with directly affects mankind. Another trait of the classicist is his hatred of extremes. Goldsmith reveals this feeling in a number of ways. For example, just as in *The Traveller* he finally chooses England as the best of countries, we find him in *Animated Nature* continually singing the praises of the temperate zone in preference to those regions where either cold or heat is too great. The meteors of the torrid zone and at the poles are terrible and of great variety; but 'in our own gentle climate, where Nature wears the mildest and kindest aspect, every meteor seems to befriend us.'[2]   In England there are no ferocious beasts and almost no venomous serpents; and even the rivers of the temperate zone are to be preferred to those of any other:

[1] 4. 353.
[2] 1. 373.

Thus, whatever quarter of the globe we turn to, we shall find new reasons to be satisfied with that part of it in which we ourselves reside. . . . The rivers of the torrid zone, like the monarchs of the country, rule with despotic tyranny, profuse in their bounties, and ungovernable in their rage. The rivers of Europe, like their kings, are the friends, and not the oppressors of the people; bounded by know[n] limits, abridged in the power of doing ill, directed by human sagacity, and only at freedom to distribute happiness and plenty.[1]

The poles are even worse than the tropics; for ' nothing can be more mournful or hideous than the picture which travellers present of those wretched regions.'[2] This Europe-worship is expressed sometimes with an almost incredible complacency:

In this manner the extremes of our globe seem equally unfitted for the comforts and conveniences of life; and although the imagination may find an awful pleasure in contemplating the frightful precipices of Greenland, or the luxurious verdure of Africa, yet true happiness can only be found in the more moderate climates, where the gifts of nature may be enjoyed without incurring danger in obtaining them.

It is in the temperate zone, therefore, that all the arts of improving nature, and refining upon happiness, have been invented: and this part of the earth is, more properly speaking, the theatre of natural history. Although there be millions of animals and vegetables in the unexplored forests under the line, yet most of these may for ever continue unknown, as curiosity is there repressed by surrounding danger. But it is otherwise in these delightful regions which we inhabit, and where this art has had its beginning. Among us there is scarce a shrub, a flower, or an insect, without its particular history; scarce a plant that could be useful which has not been propagated; nor a weed that could be noxious which has not been pointed out.[3]

[1] I. 226.

[2] I. II.

[3] I. 14-15. Examination of eighteenth century menus will show how *few* palatable vegetables were cultivated. Like the old woman, ' victuals and drink were the chief of their diet,' ' the victuals ' being usually flesh.

But, just as we should expect from the patriotic author of *The Traveller*, England is the final goal for the seeker after comfort and contentment :

> Happy England ! where the sea furnishes an abundant and luxurious repast, and the fresh waters an innocent and harmless pastime ; where the angler, in cheerful solitude, strolls by the edge of the stream, and fears neither the coiled snake, nor the lurking crocodile ; where he can retire at night, with his few trouts, to borrow the pretty description of old Walton, to some friendly cottage, where the landlady is good, and the daughter innocent and beautiful ; where the room is cleanly, with lavender in the sheets, and twenty ballads stuck about the wall ! There he can enjoy the company of a talkative brother sportsman, have his trouts dressed for supper, tell tales, sing old tunes, or make a catch ! There he can talk of the wonders of Nature with learned admiration, or find some harmless sport to content him, and pass away a little time, without offence to God, or injury to man ! [1]

Some of the most striking passages of *Animated Nature* deal in a neo-classic way with gentle landscapes, or wild, remote, and therefore hideous ones :

> When we take a slight survey of the surface of our globe, a thousand objects offer themselves, which, though long known, yet still demand our curiosity. The most obvious beauty that every where strikes the eye is the verdant covering of the earth, which is formed by an happy mixture of herbs and trees of various magnitudes and uses. [2]

Then, after an enumeration of the delightful things in nature comes :

> Such are the most obvious and tranquil objects that every where offer : but there are others of a more awful and magnificent kind ; the *Mountain* rising above the clouds, and topt with snow ; the *River* pouring down its sides, encreasing as it runs, and losing itself, at last, in the ocean ; the *Ocean* spreading

[1] 6. 345.
[2] 1. 15.

its immense sheet of waters over one half of the globe, swelling
and subsiding at well-known intervals, and forming a communi-
cation between the most distant parts of the earth.[1]

Mountains, in particular, arouse Goldsmith's wonder :

> In this survey [of the surface of the earth], its mountains
> are the first objects that strike the imagination, and excite
> our curiosity. There is not, perhaps, any thing in all Nature
> that impresses an unaccustomed spectator with such ideas of
> awful solemnity, as these immense piles of Nature's erecting,
> that seem to mock the minuteness of human magnificence. . . .
> Even among us in England, we have no very adequate ideas
> of a mountain-prospect ; our hills are generally sloping from
> the plain, and clothed to the very top with verdure ; we can
> scarce, therefore, lift our imaginations to those immense piles,
> whose tops peep up behind intervening clouds, sharp and
> precipitate, and reach to heights that human avarice or curiosity
> have never been able to ascend.
>
> We, in this part of the world, are not, for that reason, so
> immediately interested in the question which has so long
> been agitated among philosophers, concerning what gave rise
> to these inequalities on the face of the globe. In our own
> happy region, we generally see no inequalities but such as
> contribute to use and beauty ; and we, therefore, are amazed
> at a question enquiring how such necessary inequalities came
> to be formed, and seeming to express a wonder how the globe
> comes to be so beautiful as we find it. But though with us
> there may be no great cause for such a demand, yet in those
> places where mountains deform the face of Nature, where they
> pour down cataracts, or give fury to tempests, there seems
> to be good reason for inquiry either into their causes or their
> uses.[2]

Here the neo-classic demand for utility is especially
evident. So I might cite many other passages—descriptions of tropic forest, deserts, arctic wastes, erupting

---

[1] I. 16.

[2] I. 136-138. Goldsmith seems a little proud of having seen
the Alps ; upon these mountains, it will be remembered, the Traveller
sat in imagination to contemplate Europe.

volcanoes,[1] hurricanes, and other such 'awful' spec-
tacles; but I think these are sufficient to illustrate
Goldsmith's attitude toward the terrible in nature.

So far it is evident that *Animated Nature* reflects
most of the popular literary tendencies of the day;
but, since these tendencies are themselves based upon
a very definite philosophy, it will be even more interesting to see what ideas Goldsmith expresses about
certain of the questions which occupied the philosophers
of his day. The first noticeable thing about Goldsmith's philosophy is that, though he has some very
definite ideas about God, yet he talks very little about
him. The key to this is found at the very beginning
of the book:

> Modern philosophy has taught us to believe, that, when
> the great Author of nature began the work of creation, he
> chose to operate by second causes; and that, suspending the
> constant exertion of his power, he endued matter with a quality
> by which the universal economy of nature might be continued
> without his immediate assistance.[2]

God is, apparently, not the ever-present God of Scrip-
ture, but a Being who has withdrawn from direct contact
with his creatures. Instead of ruling the universe by
his divine will, he has appointed *attraction* to be his
regent, and in order to retain harmony has counteracted
the first attraction

> by another power of equal efficacy; namely, a progressive
> force which each planet received when it was impelled forward,
> by the divine Architect, upon its first formation.

God's power is exerted throughout the universe; and
our globe

---

[1] Goldsmith's only illustration of inanimate nature is a most
hideous picture of an erupting volcano. (1. 87).

[2] 1. 3.

is but a small part of that great fabric in which the Deity has thought proper to manifest his wisdom and omnipotence.

Philosophers, examining the stars and planets that surround us, believe that they may perhaps be worlds like ours. Therefore,

> as the imagination also, once excited, is seldom content to stop, it has furnished each [fixed star] with an attendant system of planets belonging to itself, and has even induced some to deplore the fate of those systems, whose imagined suns, which sometimes happens, have become no longer visible.
>
> But conjectures of this kind, which no reasoning can ascertain, nor experiment reach, are rather amusing than useful. Though we see the greatness and wisdom of the Deity in all the seeming worlds that surround us, it is our chief concern to trace him in that which we inhabit.[1]

God's reasons for creating all this, however, must be left undiscovered. Indeed, he seems to hide them from the curiosity of man:

> All these [wonders of the sea's bottom] are almost wholly hid from human curiosity: the miracles of the deep are performed in secret.[2]

Volcanoes, also,

> must . . . be supplied from the deeper regions of the earth; those undiscovered tracts where the Deity performs his wonders in solitude, satisfied with self approbation![3]

Now this work of his, though it may appear rather imperfect as we see it on the earth, is a marvelous piece of perfection:

> Whenever we can examine the works of the Deity at a proper point of distance, so as to take in the whole of his design, we see nothing but uniformity, beauty, and precision. The heavens present us with a plan, which, though inexpressibly

[1] I. 6.
[2] I. 288.
[3] I. 103.

magnificent, is yet regular beyond the power of invention. Whenever, therefore, we find any apparent defects in the earth, which we are about to consider, instead of attempting to reason ourselves into an opinion that they are beautiful, it will be wiser to say, that we do not behold them at the proper point of distance, and that our eye is laid too close to the objects to take in the regularity of their connexion. In short, we may conclude, that God, who is regular in his great productions, acts with equal uniformity in the little.[1]

Having now convinced himself that the ' best of all possible worlds ' lies before him, Goldsmith is confronted with the difficulty of accounting for the evil in it. The good things are easily apparent. The earth, being placed at just the right distance from the sun,

seems in a peculiar manner to share the bounty of the Creator : It is not, therefore, without reason that mankind consider themselves as the peculiar objects of his providence and regard.[2]

It is not right, however, thinks Goldsmith, to silence inquiry as to the reason for the existence of a thing

by alleging the benefits we receive from [it], instead of investigating the cause of its production. If I enquire how a mountain came to be formed, such a reasoner, enumerating its benefits, answers, because God knew it would be useful. . . . Those men who want to compel every appearance and every irregularity in Nature into our service, and expatiate on their benefits, combat that very morality which they would seem to promote. God has permitted thousands of natural evils to exist in the world, because it is by their intervention that man is capable of moral evil; and he has permitted that we should be subject to moral evil, that we might do something to deserve eternal happiness, by shewing that we had rectitude to avoid it.[3]

---

[1] i. 7-8. Gulliver, one recalls, remarked the unpleasant effect of too close inspection in the case of the complexion of his people of Brobdingnag, but, of course, drew exactly the opposite conclusion.

[2] i. 9.

[3] i. 19-20.

The most rational answer, therefore, why either mountains
or plains were formed, seems to be, that they were thus fashion-
ed by the hand of Wisdom, in order that pain and pleasure
should be so contiguous as that morality might be exercised
either in bearing the one, or communicating the other.[1]

It is indeed amazing to contemplate the strange things
God may be considered as doing under this plan :

The inhabitants of India, says a modern philosopher [Linnæus],
sustain an unceasing languor, from the heats of their climate,
and are torpid in the midst of profusion. For this reason,
the great Disposer of Nature has clothed their country with
trees of an amazing height, whose shade might descend from
the beams of the sun ; and whose continual freshness might,
in some measure, temperate their fierceness.[2]

We have seen the benefits man may derive even from
the savage beasts ; God has wisely given man

many opponents, that might at once exercise his virtues, and
call forth his latent abilities.[3]

Meteors, also, seem great evils :

These, however, are terrors that are seldom exerted in our
mild climates. They only serve to mark the page of history
with wonder ; and stand as admonitions to mankind, of the
various stores of punishment in the hands of the Deity, which
his power can treasure up, and his mercy can suspend.[4]

And even if death be cited as an indubitable evil,

it may be answered, that [man's term of life] was abridged
by Divine Command, in order to keep the earth from being
overstocked with inhabitants.[5]

[1] I. 139. I have myself heard the doctrine of these two quotations expounded from more than one pulpit.

[2] I. 324.

[3] 2. 9.

[4] I. 376.

[5] 2. 203. War has more than once been argued for, *nostrâ
memoriâ*, by this same reasoning.

There can be little doubt, I think, that this conception of God is fundamentally deistic, though Goldsmith would strongly have objected to such a term. The difficulty about the conception is that, by placing God at such a distance, we are somewhat at a loss when we want to speak of the more minute happenings of the natural world. To supply this lack, Goldsmith adopts the word ' Nature,' and uses it in a variety of vague and concrete senses. Sometimes he varies it by using ' Providence,' which very occasionally means almost ' God,' though usually it seems synonymous with ' Nature.' The rapid growth in popularity of this word ' Nature ' in the eighteenth century, as rationalism gradually drove out the word ' God ' except in a very restricted sense, is a most interesting indication of the fact that, while systems of philosophy may juggle with words, they can seldom change man's fundamental conceptions. The idea of God—the first cause and immanent power of the universe—suffers very little change in the mind of the religious man—and there are few men who are not at bottom religious—whether he express it in terms of the Christian Trinity, or in what might be called the Duality which rationalism set up in its place. Goldsmith is fundamentally religious ; and though he defines his God by the terms of deism, he nevertheless needs what he calls ' Nature ' to complete the conception. Goldsmith's ' Nature ' is simply God as he is manifested in the working of natural laws ; and the great principle upon which Nature works is that of compensation. Just as the law of gravitation is a law of balance, so every good or ill in nature is balanced by an equal and opposite good or ill. To compensate for the swallowing up of land by earthquakes and tidal waves, Nature produces new lands by the use of the same subterranean fires that caused the apparent

i

calamities.[1]   All nature is thus in continual fluctuation :

> The transmigration of souls is no doubt false and whimsical ;
> but nothing can be more certain than the transmigration of
> bodies : the spoils of the meanest reptile may go to the formation
> of a prince ; and, on the contrary, as the poet has it, the body
> of Cæsar may be employed in stopping a beer-barrel.[2]

Even the animals have their share in this compensation :
there is scarce a quadruped,

> how rudely shaped soever, that is not formed to enjoy a state
> of happiness fitted to its nature. All its deformities are only
> relative to us, but all its enjoyments are peculiarly its own.[3]

Vegetables are destroyed to feed animals, but animal
bodies finally fertilize vegetable life. The very dispositions of animals are part of the general scheme :
' It is a rule that obtains through Nature, that the
smallest animals multiply the fastest.'[4] This is a wise
provision, which serves to keep the weak on a par with
the strong. By the same rule, large animals usually
bring forth but one at a time ; and rapacious animals
have a certain disposition which protects the rest of
animated nature :

> It is happy for the wretched inhabitants of those climates
> [Africa], that its most formidable animals are all solitary ones ;
> that they have not learnt the art of uniting, to oppress mankind ;
> but each, depending on its own strength, invades without any
> assistant.[5]

One final wise provision completes the plan of Nature.
For pure economy's sake it would not be well for any

[1] 1. 125 ff.
[2] 1. 269.
[3] 2. 313-314.
[4] 2. 333.
[5] 2. 331.

part of nature to be uninhabited. Therefore we have creatures of every possible sort, in order that they may fit into every possible corner of the earth. This sometimes seems to Goldsmith almost the only apparent reason for the existence of certain useless creatures, such as insects, deep-sea fishes, and even some quadrupeds:

> As we have seen some quadrupedes formed to crop the surface of the fields, and others to live upon the tops of trees, so the Mole is formed to live wholly under the earth, as if Nature meant that no place should be left wholly untenanted.[1]

Thus, if we combine Goldsmith's conceptions of God and of Nature, we find that, though he has adopted the terminology of rationalism, his idea of the government of the universe differs little from that of traditional Christianity.

Man is the only creature which does not fit mechanically into this scheme. Goldsmith is far from admitting that man is merely a highly developed animal, though he is of course aware of how many impulses man has in common with brutes. The very first paragraph of *Animated Nature* strikes the note which sounds through the whole book:

> The world may be considered as one vast mansion, where man has been admitted to enjoy, to admire, and to be grateful. The first desires of savage nature are merely to gratify the importunities of sensual appetite, and to neglect the contemplation of things, barely satisfied with their enjoyment: the beauties of nature, and all the wonders of creation, have but little charms for a being taken up in obviating the wants of the day, and anxious for a precarious subsistence.
>
> Our philosophers, therefore, who have testified such surprise at the want of curiosity in the ignorant, seem not to consider that they are usually employed in making provisions of a more important nature; in providing rather for the necessities than

[1] 4. 90.

the amusements of life. It is not till our more pressing wants
are sufficiently supplied, that we can attend to the calls of
curiosity; so that in every age scientific refinement has been
the latest effort of human industry.

Man, then, though he has all the imperfections of an
animal, is a creature set apart for the execution of God's
inscrutable purpose :

> The universe may be considered as the palace in which
> the Deity resides; and this earth as one of its apartments.
> In this, all the meaner races of Animated Nature mechanically
> obey him ; and stand ready to execute his commands, without
> hesitation. Man alone is found refractory; he is the only
> being endued with a power of contradicting these mandates.
> The Deity was pleased to exert superior power in creating
> him a superior being; a being endued with a choice of good
> and evil; and capable, in some measure, of co-operating with
> his own intentions. Man, therefore, may be considered as a
> limited creature, endued with powers imitative of those residing
> in the Deity. He is thrown into a world that stands in need
> of his help; and has been granted a power of producing har-
> mony from partial confusion.[1]

This conception of man is fundamentally different from
that upon which sentimentalism is based. Man is not
naturally good ; he merely has the power to become so.
Goldsmith has no illusions about the ' natural ' man.
The ' gentle savage ' is, as we shall see, ' a poor contemptible being.' We can not even be sure that this
world with all its creatures is, as we have so often been
taught to believe, created solely for our benefit.

> But of this we are certain, that God has endowed us with
> abilities to turn this great extent of waters to our own advan-
> tage. He has made these things, perhaps, for other uses ; but
> he has given us faculties to convert them to our own. This
> much agitated question, therefore, seems to terminate here.
> We shall never know whether the things of this world have
> been made for our use ; but we very well know, that we have

[1] I. 396.

been made to enjoy them. Let us then boldly affirm, that
the earth, and all its wonders, are ours ; since we are furnished
with powers to force them into our service. Man is the lord
of all the sublunary creation ; the howling savage, the winding
serpent, with all the untameable and rebellious offspring of
Nature, are destroyed in the contest, or driven at a distance
from his habitations. The extensive and tempestuous ocean,
instead of limiting or dividing his power, only serves to assist
his industry, and enlarge the sphere of his enjoyments. Its
billows, and its monsters, instead of presenting a scene of terror,
only call up the courage of this little intrepid being ; and the
greatest dangers that man now fears on the deep, is [*sic*] from
his fellow creatures. Indeed, when I consider the human
race as Nature has formed them, there is but very little of the
habitable globe that seems made for them. But when I consider them as accumulating the experience of ages, in com-
manding the earth, there is nothing so great, or so terrible.
What a poor contemptible being is the naked savage, standing
on the beach of the ocean, and trembling at its tumults ! How
little capable is he of converting its terrors into benefits ; or
of saying, Behold an element made wholly for my enjoyment !
He considers it as an angry deity, and pays it the homage
of submission. But it is very different when he has exercised
his mental powers ; when he has learned to find his own superiority, and to make it subservient to his commands. It is then
that his dignity begins to appear, and that the true Deity
is justly praised for having been mindful of man ; for having
given him the earth for his habitation, and the sea for an
inheritance.[1]

Thus, in a broader sense than if we considered everything as contributory to man's physical happiness, we
find that the world is perfectly suited to the moral
well-being of man :

> A world thus furnished with advantages on one side, and
> inconveniences on the other, is the proper abode of Reason,
> is the fittest to exercise the industry of a free and a thinking
> creature. These evils, which Art can remedy, and Prescience
> guard against, are a proper call for the exertion of his faculties ;

[1] I. 230-232.

and they tend still more to assimilate him to his Creator. God beholds, with pleasure, that being which he has made, converting the wretchedness of his natural situation into a theatre of triumph; bringing all the headlong tribes of Nature into subjection to his will; and producing that order and uniformity upøn earth, of which his own heavenly fabric is so bright an example.[1]

When *Animated Nature* is analyzed in this manner, the reasons for its popularity become perfectly clear. Being wrapped up in a cloak of erudition, and being written in an elegant (though certainly not accurate) style, it suited the taste of those of a neo-classic turn of mind. Replete also with all the external manifestations of sentimentalism, it appealed to that large public which had come to like a sort of refined 'nature-faking.' Its air of profound philosophy in a sugar-coating— though this philosophy was most of it borrowed, and some of it self-contradictory—exactly suited an age which was already considering philosophy as the occupation of idlers lolling on mossy banks, or ensconced, like Rousseau, in ' wild retreats.' Nevertheless, under all this trashy exterior, there is something better. The personality of a careless, but tender-hearted and well-disposed man shines through even the worst of it. There is an innate righteousness in Goldsmith's statement of his simple and, if you will, rather childish philosophy that not only charms the reader, but makes him finally admire the man himself.[2] These are the qualities, as it seems to me, that made it possible for a publisher, in spite of all the revolutionary changes

[1] I. 400.

[2] What seems to me Goldsmith's own philosophy is expressed only rarely after the third volume. As his writing becomes less careful—for it certainly does toward the end—the ideas seem less and less his own, and more and more the unthinking reflection of popular taste.

in scientific knowledge that had taken place, to risk publishing an edition of *Animated Nature* more than a century after Goldsmith's death.

This study of *Animated Nature* confirms rather than changes the accepted opinions about Goldsmith, thus putting them upon a basis of fact rather than fancy. It does, however, make necessary a certain change of emphasis in our consideration of him. Goldsmith's too great sensibility and his indolence led him into generous folly on the one hand, and thoughtless folly on the other; nevertheless, as a literary artist, though habitually careless, he was always brilliant, and endowed with a remarkable feeling for literary form. The custom has always been, just as it was among his contemporaries, to consider him as a fool, who, by some miracle, was enabled to write like a genius. The truth is that he was a genius—a much greater genius than most of his contemptuous acquaintances—who, because of an unfortunate temperament, native indolence, and 'scurvy circumstances,' was often impelled to act and talk like a fool. Moreover, much of his so-called folly would have passed for good-natured fooling among men less solemnly witty than most of his friends. To repudiate, however, as malicious or unsympathetic all the ridiculous anecdotes told of him would be just as erroneous also; *Animated Nature* shows many traces of the same thoughtlessness that is evident in the stories. One is forced finally to return to the opinion of Dr. Johnson, realizing that it is based not upon prejudice, but upon profound observation of Goldsmith's character: [1]

> Nay, Sir, the partiality of his friends was always against him. It was with difficulty we could give him a hearing. Goldsmith

---

[1] Boswell, *Life* 3. 286-287.

had no settled notions upon any subject; so he talked always
at random. It seemed to be his intention to blurt out whatever was in his mind, and see what would become of it. He
was angry, too, when catched in an absurdity; but it did not
prevent him from falling into another the next minute. . . .
Goldsmith, however, was a man, who, whatever he wrote,
did it better than any other man could do. He deserved
a place in Westminster-Abbey, and every year he lived, would
have deserved it better. He had, indeed, been at no pains
to fill his mind with knowledge. He transplanted it from one
place to another; and it did not settle in his mind; so he could
not tell what was in his own books.

Nothing could describe *Animated Nature* better than
this: it is transplanted knowledge. The remarkable
thing is that the tree flourishes so well as to appear
indigenous. No one knew better than Johnson the
faults of his friend; but no one could better appreciate
his genius. It was Johnson who cried: ' Sir, he knows
nothing; he has made up his mind about nothing;' it
was Johnson, too, who wrote the stately epitaph, with
its ' Nullum quod tetigit non ornavit: sive risus essent
movendi, sive lacrymæ;' but better than any epitaph is
the Doctor's wise and kindly word: ' Let not his frail-
ties be remembered; he was a very great man.

APPENDIX

I. Main Sources

Académie Royale des Sciences, Mémoires. 1666-.

This series is frequently mentioned, and Goldsmith certainly knew parts of it; but it is impossible to separate first-hand from second-hand references.

ADANSON, MICHEL, *A Voyage to Senegal, the Isle of Goree and the River Gambia.* (*Translated from the French.*) *With notes by an English gentleman who resided some time in that country.* London, 1759.

1. 13 ; 5. 61, 352 ; 7. 31.

ALEMBERT, JEAN LE ROND D', *Essai d'une Nouvelle Théorie de la Résistance de Fluides.* Paris, 1744.

In his discussion of hydraulics (1. 185 ff.), Goldsmith says he is following d'Alembert's *Essai.*

ANDERSON, JOHANN (Burgomaster of Hamburg), *The Natural History of Iceland, by N. Horrebov. . . . Interspersed with an account of the Island by Mr. Anderson.* 1758.

6. 195, 199, 321, 325 ; 7. 64.

This seems to be the book Goldsmith means, though he calls it simply *The History of Greenland.* The work was originally written in German: *Herrn Johann Andersons Nachrichten von Island, Grönland, und der Straße Davis.* Hamburg, 1746. There is also a Dutch edition.

ARGENVILLE, ANTOINE JOSEPH DEZALLIER D', *La Conchy-*

---

[1] As I have explained above, Chapter II, it is often almost impossible to say whether Goldsmith's citations are at first or second hand. This list is intended to contain only works which Goldsmith knew directly. If I include too many, or exclude any real sources. I must plead aberration of judgment. The figures following each title indicate places in *A. N.* where the work is referred to.

liologie . . . avec un traité de la Zoömorphose. Paris, 1742.
7. 6, 27.

> An account of the snail. I am not altogether sure that Goldsmith knew this directly.

ARTEDI, PETRUS, *Ichthyologia, sive opera omnia de piscibus.* 1738.
6. 295—298.

BOERHAAVE, HERMANN. *Many medical works.*
1. 136, 168 ; 2. 128 ; 5. 164.

> Goldsmith probably knew Boerhaave through his medical studies. He says that Boerhave ' established his reputation in physic by uniting the conjectures of those that preceded him.'

BORLASE, WILLIAM, *The Natural History of Cornwall.* Oxford, 1758.
6. 327.

> Goldsmith quotes at length.

BOSMAN, WILLEM, *A New Description of the Coast of Guinea.* London, 1705.
4. 111, 216 ; 7. 294, 296.

> Translated from the Dutch edition, Utrecht, 1704.

BOWLKER, RICHARD, *The Art of Angling improved in all its parts.* Worcester, [1746 ?].
—— —— *The Art of Angling, and Compleat Fly-fishing.* Birmingham, [1774 ?].
6. 333.

> Goldsmith probably never saw the revised edition.

BOYLE, ROBERT, *New Experiments Physico-Mechanicall, touching the spring of the Air, and its effects (made for the most part, in a new pneumatical engine),* etc. Oxford, 1660.

> Cited many times in the first volume.

BRISSON, MATHURIN JACQUES, *Ornithologie.* Paris, 1760. 6 vols.
2. 298 ; 4. 52 ; 5. 48, 268, 272, 370, 392 ; 6. 23, 126.

> One of the main sources for the history of birds.

British Zoology. [By T. Pennant ?] London, 1763.
2. 370, 385 ; 3. 43, 109, 129, 180, 207, 286, 319, 348, 353, 365 ; 4. 31, 93, 135, 154, 177 ; 7. 105.

' To this work I am indebted for several particulars with regard to the native animals of this island.' GOLD- SMITH. This is the one important source that I have been unable to examine.

BROOKES, RICHARD, M. D., *A New and Accurate System of Natural History.* London, 1763. 6 vols.

3. 321, 371 ; 4. 37.

Goldsmith wrote introductions for this work. Almost at the moment of this final writing I have come upon an interesting compilation: *The Natural History of Insects. Compiled from Swammerdam, Brookes, Gold- smith, etc.* Perth, 1792.

BUFFON, GEORGE LOUIS LE CLERC DE, and DAUBENTON, LOUIS JEAN MARIE, *Histoire Naturelle.* Paris, 1749-.

The principal source of *Animated Nature.* There are at least 150 citations by name.

BURNETT, THOMAS, *Telluris theoria sacra. Libri duo priores, de diluvio et paradiso, [libri duo] posteriores, de confla- gratione mundi, et de futuro rerum statu.* London, 1681—89. 2 vols.

1. 22 ff., 52, 138, 230.

The first English translation was in 1691, with nu- merous others to follow.

CAIUS, Dr. JOHN, *De Canibus Britannicis,* etc. London, 1570.

3. 285—290.

The first English translation was in 1576, with later editions and translations. Goldsmith may get his knowledge of Dr. Caius through *British Zoölogy.*

CATESBY, MARK, *The Natural History of Carolina, Florida, and the Bahama Islands.* London, 1731—43.

3. 381 ; 5. 112.

A most carefully prepared book, with fine plates.

CRANTZ, DAVID, *The History of Greenland, containing a description of the country and its inhabitants and a relation of the Mission carried on for above these thirty years by the Unitas Fratrum at New Herrnhuth and Lichtenfels in that country. Translated from the High Dutch.* [Edited and in part translated by J. Gambold.] London, 1767. 2 vols.

1. 11, 225, 243—247, 325, 388—389; 2. 214, 217; 3. 46, 356; 4. 169.

DAUBENTON. *See* BUFFON.

DERHAM, WILLIAM, *Physico-Theology: or a demonstration of the being and attributes of God from his works of creation. Being the substance of XVI sermons, preached . . . at Mr. Boyle's Lectures, in the years 1711 and 1712. With notes and observations never before published.* London, 1713.
—— —— *Astro-Theology*, etc. London, 1715.

1. 199, 229, 354; 2. 29, 264; 4. 92; 7. 84, 170.

I am not certain that Goldsmith knew the *Astro-Theology*. Derham also contributed to the *Philosophical Transactions*. He was a favorite writer of Robert Burns.

EDWARDS, GEORGE, *The Natural History of Uncommon Birds.* London, 1743—51.

4. 216; 5. 141, 243; 6. 59.

A most remarkable collection of colored plates with their descriptions, more important as a source than the number of citations indicates.

FORBIN, *Mémoires du Comte de Forbin, Chef d'Escadre, Chevalier de l'Ordre Militaire de Saint Louis.* Amsterdam, 1730. 2 vols.

4. 201.

A most interesting book, with an abundance of first-hand information about Siam.

GEER, CHARLES DE, *Mémoires pour Servir à l'Histoire des Insectes.* Stockholm, 1752—78.

8. 117, 123.

GESNER, KONRAD VON, *Historia animalium.* Zurich, 1556—87. 4 vols.

3. 250, 319, 369; 4. 74, 134; 5. 329—332, 371, 375; 6. 58, 172, 275, 339; 7. 222.

GOUAN, ANTOINE, *Historia piscium, sistens ipsorum anatomen genera in classes et ordines redacta.* [Latin and Frenc Argentorati, 1770.

6. 157—158, 296—298.

Gouan's principal field was botany.

GUGLIELMINI, GIOVANNI DOMENICO, *Della Natura de Fiumi, trattato fisico-mathematico*. Bologna, 1697.

I. 200, 202, 207.

I find no English translation; Goldsmith may have used the Italian—though this is the only trace I have found of his reading Italian—since it is not in any of the sources I have looked at. However, it is quite possible that he got it somewhere at second hand.

HAMILTON, HUGH, (Successively Bishop of Cloufert and of Ossory), *Philosophical Essays. . . I. On the principles of mechanics. II. On the ascent of vapours, the formation of clouds, rain, and dew. III. . . . on the nature of the Aurora Borealis, and the tails of comets.* London, 1766.

I. 368.

Two other editions, 1767 and 1772, successively ' improved and enlarged.' Goldsmith refers to ' Dr. Hamilton of the University of Dublin.'

HERBELOT, *Bibliothèque Orientale, ou Dictionnaire Universel contenant généralement tout ce qui regarde la connoissance des peuples de l'Orient*, etc. Paris, 1697.

I. 359.

HILL, JOHN, M. D. (calling himself Sir JOHN), *Fossils arranged according to their obvious characters, with their history and description*, etc. London, 1771.

I. 45, 50, 74, 168.

If Goldsmith had executed his projected extension of the natural history into the field of fossils and vegetables, Hill's book would undoubtedly have been an important source of his information.

HOFFBERG. ' For the greatest part of this description of the rein-deer, I am obliged to a Mr. Hoffberg; upon whose authority, being a native of Sweden, and an experienced naturalist, we may confidently rely.'

3. 151 ff.

KIRCHER, ATHANASIUS, *Mundus subterraneus, in XII. libros digestus, quo divinum subterrestris mundi opificium . . . universæ denique naturæ majestas et divitiæ summæ rerum varietate exponuntur*, etc. Amsterdam, 1665. 2 vols.

KIRCHER, ATHANASIUS, *The Vulcanos: or, burning and fire-vomiting mountains, famous in the World: with their remarkables. Collected for the most part out of Kircher's " Subterraneous World."* (A partial English translation—88 pages.) London, 1699.

     1. 52, 67, 77, 84, 102, 115—121, 213, 263, 268, 293—297 ; 4. 347.

     ' The reader, I hope, will excuse me for this long translation from a favourite writer ' (1. 121). The last citation refers to *Musurgia universalis, sive ars magna consoni et dissoni.* Rome, 1650. Goldsmith elsewhere says that Kircher has set down the songs of birds in musical notation, and must be thinking of volume 1, page 30 of the *Musurgia.* The following is an example of one of the ' songs ' :

Vox parturientis Gallinæ

to to to to to to to to : | :   to to to to to to to to toto : | :

KLEIN, JACOB THEODOR, *Quadrupedum dispositio brevisque historia naturalis.* Leipzig, 1751.

     2. 294 ; 3. 16—17, 395, 399 ; 4. 25, 32 ; 5. 353 ; 6. 157 ; 7. 112.

LABAT, JEAN BAPTISTE, *Nouvelle Relation de l'Afrique Occidentale,* etc. Paris, 1728. 5 vols.

     2. 344 ; 3. 130, 217 ; 4. 220, 224 ; 5. 102, 281, 358—360 ; 6. 13—14, 54—57, 247, 288—290, 364 ; 7. 127, 185.

LE COMTE, LOUIS, *Nouveaux Mémoires sur l'État Présent de la Chine.* Paris, 1697.

—— —— *Memoirs and Observations.* [Translation.] London, 1698.

     4. 200, 221 ; 6. 67—68.

     One of the sources of *The Citizen of the World.*

LINNÆUS, CAROLUS (KARL VON LINNÉ), *Systema Naturæ per Regna Tria.* Leyden, 1735.

Amœnitates Academicæ, seu Dissertationes Variæ Physicæ, Medicæ, Botanicæ, etc. Leyden, 1749. 10 vols.

LINNÆUS, CAROLUS (KARL VON LINNÉ), *Animalium Specierum . . . Methodica Dispositio.* Leyden, 1759.
The citations are too numerous to quote.

LISLE, EDWARD, *Observations in Husbandry.* London, 1757.
3. 44, 45, 197 ; 4. 74.

LOWTH. See *Philosophical Transactions.*

MACQUER, PIERRE JOSEPH, *Elémens de Chymie-pratique,* etc. Paris, 1751. 2 vols.
1. 74.

MARTIN, BENJAMIN, *Natural History of England.* London, 1759—63.
5. 228 ; 6. 71.
This is the book, I am sure, that Goldsmith means, though he cites it as *Description of the Western Isles.* This Martin was a contributor to the general Magazine of Arts and Sciences, 1755, etc.

NEWTON, Sir ISAAC, *Optics : or a treatise of the reflections, refractions,* etc. London, 1704.
1. 274, 292.

NOLLET, JEAN ANTOINE, *Leçons de Physique Expérimentale.* Paris, 1743. 2 vols.
—— —— *Lectures in Experimental Philosophy.* [Translated by J. Colson.] London, 1752.
1. 187.
Goldsmith used the translation.

PARÆUS, AMBROSIUS (AMBROSE PARÉ), *Medical works.*
2. 279.
This is the great surgeon. Goldsmith must have studied his books. In this place he says that Paré has written a treatise on the inefficacy of mummy in medicine ; but I have not located the work.

PENNANT, T., *Synopsis of Quadrupeds.* Chester, 1771. [See also *British Zoology.*]
4. 282, 347 ; 5. 94, 370 ; 6. 30, 65, 213, 237, 242, 243, 250—253 ; 7. 145, 204—205.

Philosophical Transactions.
This is a very considerable source of the local facts in *Animated Nature.* Goldsmith refers often to an

abridgement by Lowth, but I can not find this book listed anywhere. These transactions were collections of observations and articles of many sorts, which were published periodically. There are a number of reviews of them in the various magazines; e. g., the *London Magazine*. The citations from the *Transactions* or from Lowth's abridgement in *Animated Nature* are too numerous to quote.

RAY, JOHN, *Synopsis Methodica Animalium Quatrupedem et Serpentini Generis*, etc. London, 1693.

—— —— *Synopsis Methodica Avium et Piscium.* Published posthumously. London, 1713.

See also Willughby's *Ornithology*.

2. 294 ff.; 3. 187, 257, 364, 396; 4. 34, 51, 95, 132, 156, 388; 5. 191; 7. 112, 200—201.

RÉAUMUR, RENÉ ANTOINE FERCHAULT DE, *Mémoires pour servir à l'Histoire des Insectes.* Paris, 1734—42.

—— —— *The Natural History of Bees.* [Partial translation.] London, 1744.

5. 113, 265, 352; 6. 143; 7. 17, 44, 57, 241, 262—263, 366; 8. 13, 45—46, 65 ff., 78 ff., 180.

Goldsmith probably knew the translation as well as the original.

REDI, *Opusculorum pars prior, sive experimenta circa generationem insectorum.* Amsterdam, 1686.

French translation, 1755.

—— —— *Experimenta circa res diversas naturales, speciatim illas, quas ex Indiis adferuntur.* Amsterdam, 1675.

—— —— *New Experiments upon Vipers with exquisite remedies.* London, 1673.

5. 375, 378; 6. 170, 317, 380; 7. 147, 184, 198, 299—300.

All these works were originally written in Italian. Goldsmith sometimes spells the name ' Rhedi '.

ROBINSON, BRYAN, M. D., *A Course of Lectures in Natural Philosophy.* 1739.

1. 332.

RUYSCH, FREDRIK, *Catalogus Musæi Ruyschiani, sive . . . rerum naturalium*, etc. Amsterdam, 1731.

3. 124 ; 6. 52 ; 7. 110.

Ruysch wrote also various medical works in Latin.

SCHOTT, GASPAR, *Magica universalis naturæ et artis . . . opus quadripartitum. Pars I. continet Optica. II. Acoustica. III. Mathematica. IV. Physica . . . cum figuris,* etc. Herbipoli, 1657—59.

2. 168.

It is interesting to see Goldsmith's liking for music coming up again and again. This citation concerns Schott's personal observation—'*quod oculis meis spectavi*'—of the luring of fish by music.

SEBA, ALBERTIUS, *Locupletissimi rerum naturalium thesauri accurata descriptio*, etc. [Latin and French.] Amsterdam, 1734.

3. 379 ; 7. 110, 114, 139, 147, 296.

The prefatory epistle is by Boerhaave, and part of the text by Artedi.

SWAMMERDAM, JAN, *Historia Insectorum Generalis*. Amsterdam, 1685.

6. 384 ; 7. 3, 10, 17—18, 24, 29, 233—234, 241, 273, 288 —289, 357, 366 ; 8. 5, 122—123.

Goldsmith gives (4. 299) an interesting little sketch of Swammerdam's career.

TOURNEFORT, PITTON DE, *Relation d'un Voyage au Levant*, etc. Paris, 1741.

English translation, London, 1741.

1. 63, 67, 390—393.

TREMBLEY, ABRAHAM, *Mémoires pour servir à l'histoire d'un genre de polypes d'eau douce à bras en forme de corne.* Leiden, 1747.

8. 127, 180, 185, 191.

ULLOA, GEORGE JUAN *and* ANTONIO DE, *A Voyage to South America*, etc. London, 1758.

1. 74, 99—100, 145, 146—152, 153, 215, 321, 380, 382—384 ; 2. 12, 359, 379—380, 389 ; 4. 143—144 ; 7. 136.

For discussion of this book, see above, p. 50.

WILLUGHBY, FRANCIS, *Ornithology . . . to which are added, Three Considerable Discourses, I. Of the Art of Fowling . . . II. Of the Ordering of Singing Birds. III. Of Falconry.* London, 1678.

5. 93, 124, 130, 165, 206, 267—268, 271, 314, 349—350, 370, 394—395, 397 ; 6. 8—9, 25, 30, 32, 66, 99, 117.

This is Ray's translation of Willughby's Latin notes. See above, pp. 32—35, 75—76. Goldsmith always spells the name 'Willoughby'.

WHISTON, WILLIAM, *A New Theory of the Earth,* etc. London, 1696.

1. 22, 28—33.

WHYTT, *Essay upon Vital and other Involuntary Motions.* Edinburgh, 1751.

1. 332.

WOODWARD, JOHN, *An Essay toward a Natural History of the Earth,* etc. London, 1695.

1. 22, 26 ff., 40, 42, 52, 167.

As explained above, pp. 47—49, one other very important source is some collection—or collections—of travels. It is even possible that several of the books of travel here listed came to Goldsmith through a collection.

II. Ancient Writers and Literary References

ADDISON. 1. 266—267 ; 5. 72—73, 313—314 (translation of some of his Latin verses).

ÆLIAN, *De natura animalium.*

—— *Varia historia.*

1. 61 ; 3. 256, 295—297 ; 4. 261 ; 5. 171—172, 178 ; 6. 255, 393.

APICIUS. 4. 15 ; 5. 59 ; 6. 178.

ARISTOPHANES. 3. 232—233 ; 5. 161.

' However, perhaps, the caution of Aristophanes, the comic poet, is better followed in practice, who advises us to have nothing to do with this creature, but to let the lioness suckle her own whelps.' (3. 232—233). Then the Greek follows in a note.

ARISTOTLE. 1. 104, 234; 3. 136, 181; 4. 270; 5. 83, 162, 280; 6. 65, 175, 178; 7. 12, 37.

Some of these references certainly come through other writers, as 5. 83, which comes through Willughby; but some are certainly Goldsmith's own.

ATHENÆUS ('ix. 390'). 2. 250.

BACON, Sir FRANCIS. 1. 20, 339; 6. 171.

BROWN, Sir THOMAS. 2. 26.

CICERO. 6. 140.

CURTIUS, QUINTUS. 1. 258.

DIODORUS SICULUS. 6. 393.

ECCLESIASTES, 'chap. i. ver. 5, 7, 8.' 1. 193.

ERASMUS. 4. 230.

The story of a monkey belonging to Sir Thomas More.

HESIOD. 5. 229.

LOCKE, JOHN. 2. 307; 5. 276—278.

LUCAN. 7. 199 (quotation).

MACROBIUS. 1. 242.

MILTON, *Paradise Lost.* 2. 187 (Adam); 6. 65 (Cormorant), 111 (Swan).

NEMESIANUS, M. AURELIUS OLYMPIUS. 3. 294 (Latin quotation concerning the choice of a bitch).

OVID. 3. 6 (quotation concerning the rumination of the scarus):

'At contra herbosa pisces laxantur arena
Ut scarus epastas *solus* qui ruminat escas.'
'Of all the fish that graze beneath the flood,
He only ruminates his former food.'
This translation is accepted as Goldsmith's.

PAUSANIUS. 1. 133; 8. 50.

PLINY, *Historia Naturalis.* 1. 53, 110, 162, 251; 2. 265; 3. 136, 242, 295; 4. 73, 134, 287; 5. 229, 326—327, 385; 6. 122, 124, 172, 211, 220, 255, 282, 393; 7. 11, 138, 139; 8. 180.

PLUTARCH. 5. 374; 6. 109.

POPE, ALEXANDER. 1. 143, 230; 5. 188 (quotation).

SCALIGER. 7. 351.

SHAKESPEARE.   1. 269 (*Hamlet*) ; 4. 113 (*Hamlet*) ; 5. 327 (*Romeo and Juliet*) ; 6. 37 (*Lear*).

STRABO.   2. 250.

SURREY, Lord.   3. 289.

    ' I have read somewhere that the famous poet, Lord Surry [*sic*], was the first who taught dogs to set ; it being an amusement to this day only known in England.'

THOMSON, JAMES.   6. 3.

VARRO, *De Lingua Latina*.   3. 242.

    ' Tigris vivus capi adhuc non potuit.'

VIRGIL, *Georgics*.   3. 14.

WALLER.   6. 184.

    His ' beautiful poem on the Summer Islands.'

WALTON, ISAAC.   6. 345 ; 7. 89.

Some of these references may have come through other writers, though I have rigorously excluded those of which I knew this to be the case.

III. Miscellaneous Unidentified References

' The ancients had a saying, *that as the peacock is the most beautiful among birds, so is the tiger among quadrupedes ;*' and then in a note : ' Tantem [*sic*] autem præstat pulchritudine tygris [*sic*] inter alias færas quantum inter volucres pavo.'   3. 233.

CANTON.   1. 180.

    Goldsmith speaks of his experiments in the compressibility of water, but I do not identify him.

Dr. CHENEY.   1. 182.

    I can not identify him. Goldsmith says that he had a theory that the amount of water on the earth was continually diminishing.

CLANSON, PETER, *Description of Norway*.   6. 82—87.

    I can not locate this book, nor identify the writer. Goldsmith gives a long quotation descriptive of fowling on the sea-cliffs of Norway.

' Die dench wurdige. Iwerg. Hockweit, etc. Lipsiæ, 1713.
vol. viii. page 102, seq.' 2. 253.

This is perhaps a muddled reference to some German
periodical, but I have not identified it.

EGEDE, PAUL. *History of Greenland.* 1. 386.

This is, I think, a misreference. Goldsmith either
takes his reference from Crantz, or else has confused
Paul Egede with his brother, Hans Egede, whose
Description of Greenland appeared in an English translation in 1745. I can find no works by Paul. See
above, p. 50.

The German Ephemerides. 2. 141 ; 7. 174.

This is some periodical. After a story from it, Goldsmith continues : 'What credit we are to give to this
account, I will not pretend to determine : but this may
be said, that the book from whence it is taken, has some
good marks of veracity ; for it is very learned, and very
dull, and is written in a country noted, if not for truth,
at least for want of invention.'

HUGHES, *Natural History of Barbadoes.* 8. 191.

I do not identify this writer.

JACOBSON, *History of the Feroe Islands.* 6. 81—82, 100, 206.

I do not identify this writer.

Journal Œconomique. 5. 205.

' This account of the Cock of the Woods is taken
from the Journal Œconomique, and may be relied on.'
I do not find the journal.

Nature Displayed. 1. 142.

This is probably Richard Collins' *Nature Displayed :
a Poem.* London, 1727. Collins contends that ' if
the Notions of the ancient and modern Philosophers
were unloaded of the Terms, and set in a clearer or
closer view, they would be more Instructive, and more
Entertaining,' and accordingly proceeds so to treat
them in a long poem of mediocre couplets. There is
a deal of miscellaneous information (much of it faulty)
of just the sort to suit Goldsmith's needs. Goldsmith

refers to volume three, which is probably part of the
continuation which Collins promises in the introduction
of the only copy I have seen.

LOTS, of the Academy of Stockholm.   4. 153.
    I do not find this writer, to whom Goldsmith ascribes
a description of the otter.

MAUPERTUIS.   7. 294—297.
    Experiments on scorpions.   This does not seem to
be Pierre Louis Moreau de Maupertuis, but I can find
no other possibility.

Dr. MORTIMER.   7. 207.
    A medical account of the curing of 'Wm. Oliver
of Bath, June 1, 1735,' of the bite of a viper.   I do not
locate the account.

MURALTO.   6. 267.
    Anatomy of the lamprey.   This is probably Johann
von Muralt, Professor of Medicine at Zurich about 1670
I have not located this passage.

PITFIELD.   7. 102.
    Goldsmith quotes a long passage of a letter from
Pitfield to the Bishop of Carlyle, which gives an account
of the curing of cancer by the sucking of frogs.   I can
find no trace of this letter.

RAESEL, ' of Nurembergh.'   7. 76, 87, 97.
    This book seems to have been a work on frogs, with
a number of fine plates, according to Goldsmith's description.   I can not find the book.

SMITH.   4. 111, 216 ; 8. 126.

SMITH, *History of Kerry*.   5. 91.

Dr. SMITH.   1. 264 (current in the Straits of Gibraltar).
    I have been unable to place any of these ' Smith'
references.

WOLKAMER, with note : ' Ephemerides, Dec. II. 1687,
    Observ. 224.'   7. 297.
    This ' Ephemerides ' may be the same as ' The German
Ephemerides ' above.

ORDER OF PLATES IN *ANIMATED NATURE*

Plate	Marked	Now at
Volcano	1.56	1.87
Laplander	1.346	2.213
Chinese	1.350	2.221
American	1.354	2.229
*Syagush	2.177	2.322
Zebra	2.35	2.390
*Rhinoceros	2.404	3.5
Bison	2.46	3.17
Zebu	2.54	3.23
Musk	2.86	3.88
Babyrouessa	2.142	3.192
Lion	2.153	3.213
Lioness	2.163	3.231
*Tiger	2.172	3.233
Cougar	2.170	3.244
Male Panther	2.174	3.249
Lynx	2.175	3.257
Wolf	2.211	3.309
Fox	2.217	3.331
Hyæna	2.223	3.341
Pole Cat	2.235	3.363
Squash	2.243	3.381
Civet	2.248	3.388
Squirrel	2.271	4.24
Flying Squirrel	2.272	} 4.34
Squirrel in the act of Flying	2.273	
Marmout	2.274	4.37
Agouti	2.279	4.48
Paca	2.282	4.52
Guinea Pig	2.287	4.55
Mole	2.302	4.90
Hedge Hog	2.310	4.99
Tanrec	2.311	4.105
Porcupine	2.312	4.107
Pangolin	2.317	4.119

Plate	Marked	Now at
Armadillo	2.321	4.124
Bats	2.330	4.134
Otter	2.333	4.149
Beaver	2.338	4.157
Morse	2.351	4.181
Ouran Outang	2.363	4.189
Long Armed Ape	2.364	4.198
Magot	2.365	4.207
Wanderow	2.369	4.215
Mococo	2.382	4.239
Lori	2.383	} 4.241
Opossum	2.384	
Cayopolin	2.387	} 4.248
Tarsier	2.387	
Elephant	2.390	4.252
*African (elephant in background)	1.353	4.267
Camelopard	2.411	4.298
Dromedary	3.5	} 4.302
Camel	3.7	
*Brown Bear	2.15	4.321
*White Bear	2.17	4.325
Badger	3.18	4.328
Tapir	3.20	4.331
Racoon	3.21	} 4.332
Coatimondi	3.22	
Ant Bear	3.23	} 4.338
Ant Bear	3.25	
Sloth	3.26	4.343
*Tropical Birds	3.165	5.40
Ostrich	3.61	5.49
Cassowary	3.71	5.67
Dodo	3.75	5.76
Eagle	3.81	5.87
Pondicherry Eagle	3.87	5.99

* This mark signifies that the plate breaks the order established by the markings on the plates.

Plate	Marked	Now at	Plate	Marked	Now at
King of the Vultures	3.92	5.107	1 Turbinated Shell		
Toucan Huppoo Cockatoo	3.174	5.243	2 Bivalve Shell	4.43	7.12
*Birds of Paradise Guinea Fowl	3.167	5.257	3 Multivalve Shell		
Balearic Crane White Stork	3.233	5.386	Sea Urchins . . 4.65 Sea Urchins . . 4.66		7.60
Species of the Calao	3.244	6.6	1 Bull Frog P 89¹ 2 Pipal P 96 ¹	4.89	7.75
Spoon Bill Flamingo Avoset	3.246	6.10	1 Crocodile P 95¹ 2 Crocodile's Egg P 103 ¹	4.95	7.118
Grebe Culterneb Pelican	3.268	6.40	Rattle Snake Female Viper	4.144	7.208
Sword Fish Sturgeon Salmon	3.411	6.299	Spiders Scolopendra Scorpion	4.163	7.249
Crabs	4.16	6.362	Flea Louse	4.173	7.268
Land Tortoise P 28¹ Sea Tortoise P 22¹	4.28	6.374	Beetles.	4.291	8.128
			Cuttle Fish Star Fish Sea Nettle	4.315	8.177
			Coral Plants . .	4.324	8.193

¹ These numerals follow the names on the plate, and are probably page-numbers.

BIBLIOGRAPHICAL NOTE

Of contemporary or nearly contemporary works referring to Goldsmith, Boswell's *Life of Johnson* is, with the exception of the Percy Memoir, the most important. Johnson's and Boswell's letters [1] are also valuable. In addition to these there are various other volumes of memoirs and letters which give occasional anecdotes, such as Garrick's *Correspondence*, Stockdale's *Memoirs*, Walpole's *Memoirs* Walpole's *Letters*, Cradock's *Memoirs*, etc. Cradock, in particular, a very good friend of Goldsmith, relates some especially important details. These books, unfortunately, are without indexes; but Goldsmith's biographers seem to have missed nothing of consequence in them.

The best biography of Goldsmith is still that by James Prior (London, 1837). Forster imparted a more literary tone to Prior's material, and did add some details, but Prior, being much nearer in time to Goldsmith, was able often to collect verbal testimony, and, being besides thorough and conscientious, left few stones unturned. Recent books on Goldsmith are disappointing, for their writers usually think it necessary to defend him from the 'calumnies' cast upon him by his unsympathetic friends. Moreover, they too often start out with a thesis to maintain, and therefore strain the evidence to make it fit their preconceived notions. Richard Ashe King, for example, feels that Goldsmith's apparent folly may be accounted for by a vein of delicate Irish humor too subtle for the grosser wits of his friends to appreciate. There is some truth, I think, in the idea; but with little more to begin with than this frail theory, King has written a quite unnecessary book. Walter Raleigh,

---

[1] Professor Tinker's as yet unpublished edition, to which I have had access, contains some new material.

in his *Six Essays on Johnson,* supports the same theory both more briefly and more effectively. F. Frankfort Moore, also, in a much more pretentious effort, attempts to refute the mass of contemporary evidence by making of Dr. Johnson a particularly witless Othello, and of Boswell a rather ineffectual Iago. His theory can be demolished at a blow. He has, however, succeeded in making a rather attractive, though sentimental, book, in which, by rearranging old material, he produces what is nearer a novel than a biography. His accuracy, also, is not unimpeachable. The best short life of Goldsmith is the one by Austin Dobson. It does not pretend to be anything more than a simplification of Prior and Forster; but it is readable, short, and full of exceedingly sound criticism. In an appendix, Dobson prints for the first time three new letters of Goldsmith—a most valuable addition to our knowledge, in view of the scantiness of Goldsmith's extant correspondence. His bibliography, also, is very useful.

The most nearly complete edition of Goldsmith's works is that of J. W. M. Gibbs in the Bohn Library (London, 1886–88) in five volumes. Unfortunately, this book has become very rare outside of libraries.

The periodical literature is in bulk rather large. However, having made as nearly as possible a complete bibliography of this material, upon examination I found almost nothing of any worth except the following:

CRANE, R. S. *and* SMITH, H. J., ' A French Influence on Goldsmith's *Citizen of the World.' Mod. Philol.* 19 (1921—22). 82—92.

> This paper—a sort of advance notice of a forthcoming edition—is the most significant recent piece of work. Smith had already come to the same conclusions in his still unpublished Yale dissertation.

DAVIDSON, L. J., 'Forerunners of Goldsmith's *Citizen of the World.' M. L. N.* 36 (1921). 215—220.

> The value of this paper in connection with Goldsmith is somewhat lessened by the discovery of Crane and Smith.

FERGUSON, R., 'Goldsmith and the Notions *Grille* and *Wandrer* in *Werthers Leiden.*' *M. L. N.* 17 (1902). 173—178, 206—209.

FISCHER, W., 'Goldsmiths *Vicar of Wakefield.*' *Angl.* 25 (1912). 129—208; 27 (1904). 516—554.

JERROLD, W., 'A New-found Poem of Goldsmith.' *Bookman* 40 (1914). 253—254.
The poem is given in full.

LOWES, J. L., 'Wordsworth and Goldsmith.' *Nation* 92 (1911). 289—290.
A striking (and indubitable) parallel between a passage in Wordsworth's preface to the edition of 1815, and Goldsmith's essay on *Poetry Distinguished from other Writing.*

NEUENDORFF, B., 'Goldsmiths Verlorener Roman.' *Angl.* 32 (1909). 301—346

OSGOOD, C. G., 'Notes on Goldsmith.' *Mod. Philol.* 5 (1907—8). 241—252.
Principally on *The Vicar of Wakefield.* The last paragraph is an excellent criticism of Goldsmith's style.

SPRENGER, R., 'Zwei Alte Textfehler in Goldsmiths *Vicar of Wakefield.*' *Engl. Stud.* 14 (1890). 295.

SWAEN, A. E. H., 'Fielding and Goldsmith in Leyden.' *M. L. Rev.* 1 (1905—6). 327.
Proves that Goldsmith was *not* a regular student in the University there in 1754, or at any other time.

THOMAS, W. M., 'Copyright and Publication of *The Vicar of Wakefield.*' *Athen.* 2 (1885). 808—835.

There are also four German dissertations, which I have not read, but which probably contain interesting material:

LEICHSERING, A. S. C., *Über das Verhältnis von Goldsmiths She Stoops to Conquer zu The Beaux Stratagem.* Cuxhaven, 1909.

MENDT, B. A., *Goldsmith als Dramatiker.* Leipzig, 1911.

NEUENDORFF, B., *Entstehungsgeschichte von Goldsmiths Vicar of Wakefield.* Berlin, 1903.

SOLLAS, H. B. C., *Goldsmiths Einfluß in Deutschland im 18. Jahrhundert*. Heidelberg, 1903.

Of works dealing with the general period, Leslie Stephen's *History of English Thought in the 18th Century* is exceedingly helpful, as well as Texte's *Rousseau et l'Esprit Cosmopolitain*. Numerous other works on phases of sentimentalism and romanticism have been of assistance to me. In the field of the drama, I have found Bernbaum's *Drama of Sensibility*, and G. Lanson's *Nivelle de la Chaussée et la Comédie Larmoyante* particularly helpful; and Bernbaum's *Anthology of 18th Century Poetry* has an excellent introduction, in addition to being a very well arranged selection. The bibliographies in the *Cambridge History of English Literature* and that in Babbitt's *Rousseau and Romanticism* are good—the best I have found covering this whole period.

INDEX